DECLARE IT

DECLARE IT

Includes Declarations for 96 Different Life Situations

STEVE BACKLUND

Copyright © 2022 by Steve Backlund and Tracy Rice.

ISBN: 978-1-7363601-4-9

All rights reserved. No part of this book may be reproduced or transmitted in any form or by any means, electronic or mechanical, including photocopying, recording, or by any information storage and retrieval system, without permission in writing from the copyright owner.

This book was printed in the United States of America.

CONTENTS

Introduction 11

1. **MY MIND** 13
   Memory 13
   Continually Learning 14
   Improving Your Beliefs 15
   Thought Life 16
   Wisdom 17
   Creativity 18

2. **MY WILL** 19
   Obedience 19
   Humility 20
   Being A Powerful Person (Inspired by Keep Your Love On!) 21
   Overcoming Temptation 22
   Growth and Change 23

3. **MY EMOTIONS** 24
   Victorious Emotions 24
   Hope/Optimism 25
   Joy 26
   Courage 27
   Peace 28
   Caring for My Heart 29
   Freedom From Fear 30

4. **MY SPIRIT** 31
   Spirit Awareness 31
   Power of the Holy Spirit 33
   Gifts of the Holy Spirit 34

    Dreaming... 35
    Grow in Faith 36
    Hearing God 37

5. **MY IDENTITY** **38**
    Who I Am 38
    Confidence 39
    Loved By God 40
    Freedom From Fear of Rejection 41

6. **MY PURPOSE** **42**
    My Future 42
    Having Strong Convictions 43

7. **SPIRITUAL PRACTICES** **45**
    Reading The Bible 45
    Powerful Prayers 46
    Thankfulness 47
    Evangelism Part 1 48
    Evangelism Part 2 49

8. **WORSHIP** **50**
    My Worship 50
    Worship Leading 51
    Leading a Team 52
    Spontaneous Worship 53

9. **RELATIONSHIPS** **54**
    Walking in Love 54
    Difficult Relationships 55
    Conflict Resolution 56
    Unbelievers (Part 1) 57
    Unbelievers (Part 2) 58
    The Words I Speak 59
    Patience 60

10. FAMILY RELATIONSHIPS 61
Future Spouse (Part 1) 61
Future Spouse (Part 2) 62
My Marriage (Part 1) 63
My Marriage (Part 2) 64
Children / Parenting (Part 1) 65
Children / Parenting (Part 2) 66
Parenting Grown Children 67
Relationships with My Parents 68
Spiritual Parents 69
Pregnancy 70

11. PHYSICAL BODY 71
Healthy Body 71
Healing 72
Sleep 73
Weight Loss 74
Energy 75

12. FINANCES 76
Mindset of Abundance 76
Financial Abundance 78
Generosity 79
Debt 80

13. DAILY LIFE 81
Favor on My Life 81
Today's Favor 82
Decision Making 83
Time Management 84
Travel 85
Safety 86
Meetings 87
Responsibilities 88
Job Success 89

14. MY LEADERSHIP 90
Empowerment Part. 1
(Inspired by The Culture of Empowerment) 90
Empowerment Part. 2
(Inspired by The Culture of Empowerment) 91
Authority 92
Influence Part. 1 93
Influence Part. 2 94
Character 95
Meetings I Lead 96

15. OUR CHURCH 97
Favor In Our City 97
Unity 98
Hunger and Revival 99
Serving 100
Church Finances 101
Leadership Team 102

16. SPECIFIC LIFE CHALLENGES 103
Overcoming The Past 103
Unexpected Difficulty/Disappointment 104
Lingering Illness 105
Anxiety/Depression 106
Overcoming Addictions 107

17. PERSONAL DECLARATIONS 108
Tips For Writing Declarations 108
Prophetic Words 109
Promises 109
Breakthrough Areas 109

18. MORE RESOURCES 112

ACKNOWLEDGEMENTS

Tracy Rice, Ash Anderson, Annalisa Gilbert, and Lauren Chen

INTRODUCTION

What are declarations?

Declarations are biblically-based faith statements about God's promises, our identity, and our abilities. It is a practical way to implement the Romans 4:17 principle of bringing life to seemingly dead areas in our lives by "calling those things that do exist as though they did." They are an expansion of Joel 3:10 – "Let the weak SAY, 'I am strong.'"

Declaring truth is a major step in moving our prayer life from begging and unbelief into confidence and faith. "Now this is the confidence that we have in Him, that if we ask anything according to His will, He hears us. And if we know that He hears us, whatever we ask, we know that we **have** the petitions that we have asked of Him" (1 John 5:14-15). Declaring we have something before it is in our experience is a demonstration we believe our prayers are answered.

Declarations help us live out Proverbs 18:21 – "Life is in the power of the tongue." Jesus came to give us abundant life (John 10:10). The level of life we experience is greatly dependent on the amount of life we speak. Declarations are a main way to speak life.

Declarations are a main way we renew our minds and see transformation. "Be transformed by the renewing of your mind" (Romans 12:2) Through declarations intentionally speaking God's truth aloud over ourselves, circumstances, people we love, etc., God has given us a powerful, effective tool to renew our minds. And because "faith comes by hearing" (Romans 10:17), declarations have the power to increase our level of faith to propel us to experience all that Jesus has won for us.

I (Steve), carry around a declaration clicker (tally counter) and purpose to make at least 100 faith declarations a day about God's promises, my biblical identity, prayers I have prayed, and the increase of blessings. It is life-changing! A lot of what my wife, Wendy, and I are experiencing today is the result of declarations we spoke 25 years ago when it seemed ridiculous to believe for such things.

This book, *Declare It*, is a gold mine of truth to declare. Why don't you do an experiment of making at least 100 declarations a day for a month? You can start in the beginning of the book, or you can find topics that are especially timely to focus on.

As an added resource, we encourage you to check out Steve's book, *Declarations*, for a more-in depth understanding of this subject (including 30 biblical reasons for making declarations, answers common objections to making declarations, and deeper teachings on the power of what we intentionally speak).

We bless you as you use this book to bring breakthrough to you and others.

MY MIND

Memory

1. My brain is functioning at a stronger level every day.
2. I am known for my sharp memory, and others rely on me to remember facts.
3. I consistently remember important dates and appointments.
4. I consistently think with clarity.
5. My IQ is supernaturally improving.
6. I store new facts efficiently.
7. I can easily recall Scriptures I've read, and it is easy for me to memorize the Bible.
8. I have a clear, focused, and sharp mind.
9. My memory is improving as I get older.
10. I am increasingly taking advantage of the full capacity and ability of my mind.
11. I have an unusual ability to remember where I have placed things.
12. I remember names of people well.
13. I have the mind of Christ (1 Corinthians 2:16), and my brain is constantly influenced by His Presence.
14. I remember small details and desires expressed by the important relationships in mylife.
15. I remember seemingly random facts that are always end up being useful and relevant.

DECLARE IT

Continually Learning

1. God has given me extraordinary wisdom, understanding, and knowledge. (James 1:5, 2 Corinthians 2:7)
2. Like the Hebrew children in Daniel 1, I have ten times greater wisdom because of my relationship with God.
3. My mind is being renewed to think in powerful ways. (Romans 12:2)
4. I am highly intelligent and have brilliant, solution-focused thoughts all the time.
5. I have a high capacity to learn, and it is easy for me to learn new things.
6. I grasp new or seemingly difficult concepts easily.
7. I excel in educational and academic environments.
8. Brilliant, societal-transforming thinkers are in my lineage.
9. My descendants include authors, scientists, inventors, teachers, innovators, and great leaders.
10. I walk in revelation knowledge concerning all matters in life.
11. I am able to learn in many different ways.
12. I never waste a mistake or challenge but always learn something new about myself, others, and God.
13. I am a lifelong learner.
14. I am knowledgeable in a wide variety of fields.
15. I am known for my strong, sharp intellect.

Notes

_____

_____

_____

_____

_____

_____

Improving Your Beliefs

1. I have the mind of Christ and think as Jesus thinks. (1 Corinthians 2:16)
2. Because faith comes by hearing, I daily speak God's promises. (Romans 10:17)
3. I am being transformed by the renewing of my mind. (Romans 12:2)
4. Just as Abraham was on a journey to become fully convinced about what God said, I too am growing toward fully believing His promises.
5. I recognize every belief that does not have hope attached to it is under the influence of a lie.
6. I filter what I see, hear, and believe through the promises of God.
7. I easily recognize lies I am believing and quickly displace them with the truth.
8. My subconscious beliefs are adjusting to come into agreement with the Word of God.
9. It doesn't take long for me to renew my mind with correct beliefs.
10. I refuse to let a wrong belief go unchallenged.
11. New strongholds of truth are being built in my mind.
12. My beliefs are a great source of hope and joy.
13. My right beliefs are seen in my words and actions.
14. I pay attention to what my emotional responses tell me about what I am believing.
15. How I believe brings pleasure to God and attracts His favor.

Notes

Thought Life

1. I consistently think about what is true, of good report, and virtuous. (Philippians 4:8)
2. I have a sound mind and am known as a incredible thinker. (2 Timothy 1:7)
3. I take every thought captive to the obedience of Christ. (2 Corinthians 10:5)
4. I am a person of radical biblical optimism. (Hebrews 10:23)
5. God partners with my powerful thinking to accomplish great things.
6. My thought life is deeply connected to my identity in Christ.
7. My mind is sharp and clear, free of any confusion.
8. I am intentionally building healthy strongholds in my mind.
9. My clear thinking and positive beliefs affect everyone around me and influence chaotic atmospheres in a powerful way.
10. My imagination is sanctified by the Holy Spirit. (Romans 8:2-5)
11. I am always imagining good things happening and the best possible outcomes.
12. My thoughts are free from fear or anxiety.
13. My mind is set on things above and not on the things of earth. (Colossians 3:2)
14. My thoughts are influenced by Holy Spirit. I have the mind of Christ. (1 Corinthians 2:16)
15. I see people according to their future, not their past.

Notes

_____

_____

_____

_____

_____

_____

_____

MY MIND

Wisdom

1. I always know what to do.
2. Like Solomon, I have astounding wisdom that creates prosperity, excellence, and positively influences the life quality of multitudes.
3. My wisdom is pure, peaceable, gentle, willing to yield, full of mercy and good fruits, without partiality, and without hypocrisy. (James 3:17-18)
4. I have the wisdom of God today for whatever I face. (1 Corinthians 2:16)
5. I always have supernatural ideas and divine strategies.
6. I am pursued by leaders and influencers because of the heavenly wisdom I carry.
7. God is revealing to me surprising solutions for long-standing concerns in my life.
8. I know what to do, when to do it, and how to do it.
9. I have insight and solutions for "impossible situations."
10. I have a great perspective of the bigger picture of what God is doing.
11. I am consistently gaining wisdom and understanding of what the Kingdom of Heaven looks like.
12. I ask great questions that inspire others and diffuses tense situations.
13. I have the Spirit of wisdom and revelation living inside of me.
14. I am slow to speak and look for deeper insights.
15. My wisdom positions me for breakthrough and favor.

Notes

_____

_____

_____

_____

_____

_____

DECLARE IT

Creativity

1. I am a highly creative person because I am made in the image of Creator God.
2. I have creative, original ideas that no one has ever had before.
3. God partners with my ideas to bring freedom and breakthrough for many.
4. I have overcome any lingering lie that I am not extremely creative.
5. I have an unusual ability to establish long-lasting, life-giving structures for creative ideas.
6. I am full of supernatural ideas today.
7. My exceptional creativity manifest powerfully in my relationships, my health, my spiritual life, and in my finances,
8. I am free from regrets from the past that would hinder my creativity.
9. I am confident in expressing my creativity.
10. I do not judge my creativity based on other people's opinions.
11. I am a dreamer and my imagination is potent.
12. My imagination is the soil for divine activity today.
13. My curiosity activates greater creativity in me.
14. God wants me to thrive and use the talents that bring energy and fulfillment to my life.
15. I reveal the Holy Spirit through my creativity in a way that transforms lives.

Notes

_____
_____
_____
_____
_____
_____

MY WILL

Obedience

1. My love for God is seen in my willingness to obey. (1 John 2:3)
2. I am a doer of the Word and not just a hearer. (James 1:22)
3. God's grace on my life empowers me to obey Him in incredible ways.
4. I acknowledge God in all my ways.
5. I am responsive to His leading in my life.
6. I always obey even if it doesn't make sense or the result appears to be unfruitful.
7. I joyfully obey God from my heart and not just in my actions.
8. I respond quickly when God gives me direction.
9. It is easy for me to hear God and obey him.
10. Rebellion has no place in my heart.
11. I obey even if others do not.
12. I am convinced of God's great love for me and leap into obedience knowing Jesus came so I might have life, and life more abundantly. (John 10:10)
13. I trust God completely with every detail of my life. I say "yes" to obey Him even before I know the question.
14. I am not afraid to disappoint others if it means obeying God.
15. My acts of obedience position me for blessing and are storing up treasures in Heaven.

Humility

1. I am genuinely humble and kind.
2. I am teachable and can learn something beneficial from all people.
3. Those who humble themselves under God's mighty hand will be exalted. (1 Peter 5:6)
4. I have a natural, childlike humility. (Matthew 18:4)
5. The reward for my humility is riches, honor, and life. (Proverbs 22:4)
6. I understand the difference between true humility and the restricting effects of false humility.
7. I am always looking for ways to serve others. (Mark 10:43)
8. I intentionally surround myself with fathers, mothers, and community to give me feedback so I can keep learning and growing as a person.
9. I always see God's heart for people, and love everyone regardless of what they can offer me. (Romans 12:16)
10. I do nothing from rivalry or conceit. (Philippians 2:3)
11. I am able to rejoice when others are celebrated and promoted.
12. It is easy for me to humbly accept praise and thanks from others.
13. In humility, I forgive others, even as Christ has forgiven me.
14. God's empowering grace flows to me because of my humility. (James 4:6).
15. I am humble but confident in who I am in Christ.

Notes

_____
_____
_____
_____
_____
_____
_____

Being A Powerful Person
(Inspired by Keep Your Love On!)

1. I am a powerful person in control of my life
2. I have not been given a spirit of fear, but of power, love, and a sound mind. (2 Timothy 1:7)
3. I am not a victim, I am a victor. (1 John 5:4)
4. I have a good process of decision making and attach faith to every decision I make.
5. I take full responsibility for the choices I make in relationships based on who I am, what I want, and what I am committed to doing as an individual.
6. I do not need to be dominating in relationships to be known, seen, heard, and understood.
7. I consciously and deliberately create the environment in which I want to live.
8. I do not try to control the people around me and do a great job managing myself in my relationships.
9. I am choosing who I want to be with, what I am pursuing in life, and how I am pursuing that.
10. I empower others to be powerful around me, and I am not afraid of people bringing their full selves into.
11. I will not be controlled or respond negatively when people use withdrawal, nagging, ridiculing, pouting, crying, getting angry to pressure me, manipulation, or punishment to get me to respond.
12. I know how to create a safe place for people to know me and be known.
13. I don't base my love for people on their actions or decisions but unconditionally love others like my Father does.
14. I am not afraid of brave communication, and I know I am secure in my relationships.
15. I am very self-aware and know how I am affecting the people around me.

Overcoming Temptation

1. I have an unusual ability to overcome temptation.
2. Because I have a great vision for my life, I have no time or desire for sin.
3. Because the Son has set me free, I am free indeed. (John 8:36)
4. I do not walk according to the flesh, but according to the Spirit. (Romans 8:5)
5. I receive God's abundant provision of grace and the gift of righteousness to reign in life through Jesus Christ! (Romans 5:17)
6. Greater is He who is in me than he who is in the world. (1 John 4:4)
7. I am dead to sin and alive to obeying God and living supernaturally. (Romans 6:11; 2 Peter 1:4)
8. God is faithful and won't let me be tempted beyond my ability to overcome or escape it. (1 Corinthians 10:13)
9. God always shows up when I need His strength and truth to fight temptation.
10. I am filled with the Holy Spirit and it is natural for me to exercise self-control.
11. It becomes easier and easier for me everyday to resist temptation and live from my spirit identity.
12. I am a master at keeping my thoughts captive to the obedience of Christ to overcome any sinful thoughts.
13. I am surrounded by a community of people who love me and help keep me accountable to the standard God has called me to live.
14. I walk in vulnerability and let myself be seen and known to the people in my life who love me.
15. I have non-negotiable convictions and I am a pillar of integrity. I stand for what I believe in, no matter what I am feeling.

Growth and Change

1. "I am confident of this very thing, that He who has begun a good work in me will complete it until the day of Jesus Christ." (Philippians 1:6)
2. I am continually being changed into Christlikeness by the power of the Holy Spirit.
3. I am in a season of tremendous growth and positive change.
4. My desire to keep growing as a person positively affects everyone around me.
5. I am being transformed in my behavior by the renewing of my mind every day. (Romans 12:2)
6. I trust Father God to bring up things to change at the right time and to empower me to make those changes.
7. I readily cooperate with God who works in me to will and to act in order to fulfill His good purpose. (Philippians 2:13)
8. I love and embrace opportunities to grow!
9. I celebrate progress, not perfection.
10. My life is dramatically changing for the better because I have been blessed by God through Jesus Christ.
11. I joyfully receive correction from the Holy Spirit.
12. I am open to correction from people around me and walk in wisdom knowing what to do with the feedback I'm given.
13. Because I have a great vision for my life, I see everything in my life now as training for this vision.
14. I don't punish myself when I seemingly fail,, but I embrace Father God's love and move forward.
15. My past has no say in how much or how fast I can change.

Notes

_____

_____

_____

_____

MY EMOTIONS

Victorious Emotions

1. I am an emotionally healthy person.
2. My emotions are under the influence of unconditional love.
3. Every day, my emotions are being affected by God's love and grace, leading me into a default of hope and joy.
4. My emotions increasingly experience every aspect of salvation that Jesus won for me.
5. I love to laugh.
6. I am free from all shame and guilt.
7. My right, godly beliefs are influencing my emotions in positive ways.
8. I celebrate progress, not perfection, concerning my learning to walk in victorious emotions.
9. I have an unusual ability to help others become emotionally healthy.
10. I am able to discern which emotions are mine, and which are emotions that I'm picking up in the atmosphere around me.
11. I allow my emotions to reveal to me what I am truly believing.
12. I am healed from all negative emotional trauma I have experienced.
13. It is natural for me to have healthy emotions.
14. My family line has a blessing of healthy process and victorious emotions.
15. My emotions are always under the influence of hope and joy.

Hope/Optimism

1. Today will be the best day of my life spiritually, emotionally, relationally, and financially in Jesus' name. (Romans 15:13)
2. There is always a solution to every situation I face. (1 Corinthians 10:13)
3. I always see the goodness of the Lord around me. (Psalms 27:13)
4. I am a person of biblical optimism. (Hebrews 10:23)
5. I believe the future will be better than the present, and I have the power to help make it so.
6. The Holy Spirit lives inside of me, and He says nothing is hopeless.
7. All things in my life work together for my good.
8. My heart and mind are glistening with confident hope, joy, and positive expectation.
9. There are zero hopeless circumstances in my life.
10. I am not predestined to hardship or mediocrity.
11. I see that ALL THINGS are a possibility because I see beyond the limitations of the natural realm.
12. My spirit is one with the God of hope and therefore feels no hopelessness.
13. My right beliefs create glistening hope inside of me.
14. My hope influences people around me.
15. God is good and I eagerly anticipate His goodness in my life today.

Notes

Joy

1. I consistently activate joy and laughter in my life as a secret to my strength and longevity.
2. I rejoice in the Lord at all times. (Philippians 4:4)
3. I abound in joy! I am an outrageously joyful person.
4. Because joy is ⅓ of the kingdom (Romans 14:17), I prioritize it and make room for it in my life.
5. I realize most days it is not convenient to walk in radical joy, but I do so anyway because it is my strength, and I need strength today.
6. I don't get discouraged when I am not experiencing joy because I know I am still growing into my joyful identity.
7. I naturally know when to "weep with those who weep" and "rejoice with those who rejoice."
8. My joy and laughter are powerful weapons of spiritual warfare and help create breakthrough in my own life and the lives of those around me.
9. I reject feelings of fear and foreboding and embrace feelings of hope and joy.
10. I am building a stronghold of joy in my life.
11. I am a carrier of infectious joy, and when people get around me, they can't help but become outrageously joyful!
12. My joy level is increasing daily, and I have been created to experience fullness of joy.
13. I love to laugh out loud, and I do so frequently.
14. I enjoy every single day of my life.
15. I consistently walk in the child-like wonder and excitement of working with God, instead of working for God.

Notes

_____
_____
_____
_____

MY EMOTIONS

Courage

1. I am strong and very courageous! (Joshua 1:7)
2. I am as bold as a lion. (Proverbs 28:1)
3. I can do all things through Christ who strengthens me. (Philippians 4:13)
4. I am strong in the Lord and in the strength of His might. (Ephesians 6:10)
5. I am not afraid or dismayed because God is with me. (Isaiah 41:10)
6. I confidently say, "The Lord is my helper; I will not fear; what can man do to me?" (Hebrews 13:6)
7. I inspire others to do what they have been afraid to do.
8. I do not shrink away from challenges, but I choose to face them head-on! I run at the things that I am fearful of.
9. Fear has no hold in my life.
10. My belief in God's promises makes me courageous.
11. Every day I experience more freedom from the fear of man and the fear of failure.
12. Because God fights for me and my reward is great in heaven, I am not afraid of standing up for my faith, even if it leads to persecution.
13. My courage levels are increasing everyday.
14. I am establishing a life without fear.
15. It is more natural for me to be courageous than it is to be fearful.

Notes

_____

_____

_____

_____

_____

_____

_____

Peace

1. Because my mind it set on the Spirit, my emotions and circumstances are constantly influenced by peace. (Romans 8:6)
2. I have peace in any tribulation. (John 16:33)
3. When I speak "Peace, be still" to the areas in my life, storms are calmed and raging seas still. (Mark 4:39)
4. My peace is a powerful spiritual weapon to change circumstances.
5. My peace is increasing more and more each day.
6. I am at peace even before my circumstances change.
7. I rest in God's goodness and consistency, especially at times when I lack understanding.
8. I am known as a peace-carrier at home, in the workplace, and in all areas of my life.
9. I have a unique ability to remain peaceful, even as my responsibilities increase.
10. I do not have to strive for peace, as God has already given it to me, and it is natural for me to have.
11. Everyone around me is influenced by the peace in me, and even those who struggle
with anxiety immediately experience a dramatic increase of peace in their lives around me.
12. My home is filled with a tangible peace. When I walk in, I immediately feel at ease and calm.
13. Peace is one of my strongest weapons in prayer.
14. My heart and mind are guarded and protected by God's peace.
15. I am well able to overcome all challenges.

Notes

_____

_____

_____

_____

_____

Caring for My Heart

1. I am wholehearted and reflect that in everything I do.
2. My heart is always being drawn towards God's presence.
3. I value my heart, and so does Father God. (Proverbs 4:23)
4. My heart trusts in God fully. (Proverbs 3:5-6)
5. I am well-connected to my heart, and let it have a voice in my decisions.
6. It is easy for me to communicate the needs of my heart.
7. I am not afraid of pain, and know how to process pain when it occurs.
8. I regularly do things that bless and feed my heart., and I am able to guard my heart from things that would do damage or drain me.
9. My heart rejoices in the Father's love for me! It is easy for my heart to receive His love.
10. I am tender-hearted, kind, compassionate, and loving towards myself.
11. My heart glistens with hope about every situation I face because I am able to know the truth that my Father speaks over that situation.
12. I am able to quickly assess what is my responsibility in relationships and what is not my responsibility, soI resist all codependency in my life.
13. I never say one thing but mean something else.
14. My heart is stable and consistently increasing in joy and peace.
15. I understand and embrace what my heart is passionate about.
    I love the way God made my heart.

Notes

_____

_____

_____

_____

_____

Freedom From Fear

1. I am completely fearless. Fear has no influence on my life or on my decisions.
2. The LORD is on my side; I will not fear. What can man do to me? (Psalm 118:6)
3. I am far from oppression. I am free from fear and from terror for it does not come near me. (Isaiah 54:14)
4. I am not anxious about anything, but in everything by prayer and supplication with thanksgiving, I let my requests be made known to God. (Philippians 4:6)
5. The peace of God, which surpasses all understanding, guards my heart and my mind in Christ Jesus. (Philippians 4:7)
6. I am not frightened or dismayed, for the Lord my God is with me wherever I go. (Joshua 1:9)
7. I invite the Person of Perfect Love (Jesus Himself) to invade my heart and my life, which casts out all fear. (1 John 4:18)
8. Fear is my enemy and therefore I do not make any alliances with it. I break any alliance known or unknown that I've made with fear in Jesus' name!
9. I am not afraid of being around people who hold positions of leadership or power.
10. I do not speculate or fear what people are thinking about me.
11. I am not limited or paralyzed by fear, but rather I run at fear and do the opposite of what fear says.
12. I don't let fear determine how or when I will love people.
13. I am not afraid to talk to strangers about spiritual matters or about how Father God sees them.
14. I am not intimidated by others.
15. I have not been given a spirit of fear, but of power, love and a sound mind. (2 Timothy 1:7)

MY SPIRIT

Spirit Awareness

1. I am more spirit than flesh. (Galatians 5:25)
2. The substance of God's love and peace powerfully influences people everywhere I go. (1 John 4:4)
3. My spirit is arising within me. I can feel it and I can hear it. (Ephesians 2:4-6)
4. I am a partaker of the divine nature and I look like my Father. (2 Peter 1:4)
5. I easily rest and receive in His presence. (John 20:21-22)
6. I have great revelation on how the laws of the spirit realm work. (Romans 8:1)
7. I have unseen resources and spiritual blessings to overcome every negative circumstance. (Philippians 4:19)
8. I know my past, but I imagine my future according to the power that works in me. (Ephesians 3:20)
9. The eyes of my heart and imagination are enlightened to see the glorious inheritance and power that God has for us who believe. (Ephesians 1:18-19)
10. I am supernatural. The supernatural is not something that happens to me, it is who I am.
11. God and His realm have greater impact on my circumstances than the natural realm.
12. I am aware of the unseen realm, and I influence people and atmospheres with my spirit (I Corinthians 5:3).

13. My brain hears and responds easily to the voice of my spirit. (John 10:27)
14. Holy Spirit is communicating with my spirit today and I easily hear Him.
15. My spirit is aware of angelic activity around me.

Notes

MY SPIRIT

Power of the Holy Spirit

1. I expect to heal the sick, raise the dead, prophesy life, lead people to Christ, bring deliverance, release signs and wonders, and bless every place I go. (Book of Acts)
2. I consistently bring God encounters to other people. (Mark 16:17-18)
3. I am continually being filled with the power of the Holy Spirit.
4. I expect to have powerful, divine appointments today.
5. I earnestly desire the gifts, especially to prophesy. (I Corinthians 14:1)
6. The gifts inside of me are active and I walk in the Spirit's fullness.
7. I am stirring up the gifts of the Spirit within me today. (2 Timothy 1:6)
8. All spiritual gifts are available to me and flow through me.
9. Because Jesus went to the Father, I do even great things than He did. (John 14:12)
10. Signs and wonders follow me wherever I go.
11. I am empowered to change the world.
12. I expect to experience the supernatural today.
13. I am supernatural; therefore, I am not limited to the natural realm.
14. The people and circumstances around me are influenced by the power I carry.
15. Greater is He who is in me than He who is in the world. (I John 4:4)

Notes

_____
_____
_____
_____
_____
_____

Gifts of the Holy Spirit

1. Gifts of the Holy Spirit powerfully flow through me to bring miracles and breakthrough in the lives of multitudes.
2. God uses me consistently to help people be baptized in the Holy Spirit. (Acts 1:8)
3. I operate in the gifts of healing, miracles, prophecy, and gift of faith.
4. I earnestly desire spiritual gifts, especially the gift of prophecy. (1 Corinthians 14:1)
5. Love compels me to share what Father God thinks about the people in my life. (1 Corinthians 13)
6. It is easy to prophesy and get words of knowledge for people.
7. I am empowered by the Holy Spirit to do supernatural things.
8. I operate in the gift of tongues and in the interpretation of tongues.
9. I receive detailed insights about people, situations, and God's perspectives.
10. I have an unusual ability to help others function in the gits of the Holy Spirit.
11. My spirit is able to discern what is happening in the supernatural.
12. God shows me how to release healing and deliverance to people, and miracles happen regularly through me.
13. My spirit is quickened with excitement to demolish sickness and bondage.
14. The gifts are growing and increasing in me.
15. I have great revelation from the Book of Acts and I Corinthians 12 & 14 about the gifts of the Holy Spirit.

Notes

_____

_____

_____

_____

_____

Dreaming

1. Whenever I sleep, my sleep is sweet. (Proverbs 3:24)
2. My mind moves towards Father God as I am falling asleep. (Isaiah 26:3)
3. My spirit is open to the Holy Spirit and the heavenly realm while I sleep.
4. I access the secrets of heaven while I am asleep.
5. God regularly speaks to me in dreams.
6. I get excited to go to sleep to hear what God has to say to me.
7. My room is full of peace and the Presence of God.
8. I discover Father God's heart while I'm sleeping.
9. I get insights into who I am and how Father God sees me when I dream.
10. My dreams are prophetic, and I dream in full detail.
11. I easily discern spiritual dreams from natural dreams.
12. I get solutions to problems when I dream.
13. I clearly remember my dreams and have divine wisdom in interpreting them.
14. My dreams are full of God's glory and they are beautiful.
15. I inspire and cause others to have a supernatural dream life.

Notes

Grow in Faith

1. Jesus is the author and finisher of my faith. (Hebrews 12:2)
2. My faith is the substance of things I am hoping for. (Hebrews 11:1)
3. Just like Abraham, I am on a journey of being strengthened in faith until I am fully convinced about what God has said to me. (Romans 4:20-21)
4. Because I know faith comes by hearing, I radically make declarations about the promises of God and what my identity is in Him. (Romans 10:17)
5. I live by faith, not by what I see. (2 Corinthians 5:7)
6. Faith begins where the will of God is known. (I John 5:14-15) I have a great revelation on what the will of God is.
7. I believe that whatever I ask for in faith, I will receive it at. (Mark 11:24)
8. I get excited when I am challenged to believe because it build perseverance in me! (James 1:3)
9. I overcome every obstacle and challenge by my faith. (1 John 5:4)
10. Because I have faith, I say to mountains, 'Move from here to there,' and it will move. (Matthew 17:20)
11. I do not waver in unbelief about the promise of God but am strengthened in faith, giving glory to God. I am fully convinced that what God promised, He is also able to do. (Romans 4:20-21)
12. I attach great faith to everything I do; therefore, everything I do creates life and change.
13. I have legal access by faith into heavenly places. Every time I step out in faith, I grow in my awareness of God's love.
14. I am not afraid of taking risks, even if I don't see the outcome.
15. My faith is growing day by day.

Notes

_____

_____

_____

Hearing God

1. I have an unusual ability to hear and understand what God is saying.
2. The eyes of my heart are well trained to see the unseen. (Ephesian 1:18)
3. It has been given to me to know the mysteries of the Kingdom. (Luke 8:10)
4. I recognize the voice of God and am able to distinguish His voice from other voices.
5. Hearing God is very natural to me because I am spirit and I am united with Him.
6. When I hear God, I respond quickly.
7. My Father desires to speak to me even more than I desire to hear from Him.
8. As a child of God, it is my privilege and birthright to hear my Father's voice.
9. Whatever God says to do is the most loving, most fruitful, and most exciting thing I can do.
10. I am constantly hearing God's voice through Scripture, my thoughts, other people, and nature. He never stop speaking to me!
11. Even when my mind cannot comprehend, my spirit understands what God is saying.
12. When God speaks direction to me, He also provides the grace to do what He has said.
13. As I renew my mind, God will reveal His good, pleasing, and perfect will to me.
14. Hearing God's voice and obeying in faith is worth any risk of failure.
15. I have wisdom and creative strategies to help others hear the voice of God.

Notes

_____

_____

_____

MY IDENTITY

Who I Am

1. I am a beloved child of God. (1 John 3:1)
2. I am the head, not the tail. (Deuteronomy 28:13)
3. I am who God says I am, not what my past experience says I am.
4. I can do what my Father does because I have His DNA.
5. I carry the substance of favor, and I don't need to perform for people to like me.
6. I rest in my new identity and there is no striving with it.
7. My true self is at peace with God and man.
8. I treat others based on their identity in Jesus, not how they act or treat me.
9. I am the righteousness of Christ. (2 Corinthians 5:21)
10. People see me and are drawn to the beauty of my spirit that is one with Christ.
11. I am pure in God's eyes because of the sacrifice of His son, Jesus.
12. I am 100% worthy in Jesus for all of God's blessings.
13. I am more than a conqueror. (Romans 8:37)
14. I am worthy in Jesus to see and experience the Kingdom of God.
15. I don't compare myself to others, but am comfortable being myself.

Confidence

1. Because I know who I am in Christ, and I believe God's promises, I am a confident person.
2. Because I have been with Jesus, people marvel at my boldness and confidence. (Acts 4:13)
3. God is for me today, and if God is for me, who can be against me? (Romans 8:31)
4. I trust in the Lord and will not be put to shame. (Romans 10:11)
5. I am strong and courageous. (Joshua 1:7)
6. I am completely comfortable with who I am in any situation.
7. I am not intimidated by other people.
8. I am secure and peaceful when talking to leaders and people in authority.
9. The fear of man is far from me and has no influence in my life.
10. I am a confident, influential, and joyful speaker
11. I am a good decision maker and attach confident faith to the decisions I make.
12. I always show up as the best version of myself.
13. When I walk into a room, the atmosphere shifts to peace, hope, and joy!
14. I am confident in my life assignments and in the gifts I have. I have great clarity about what I am to do and not to do.
15. I will always succeed in everything I do. (Philippians 4:11-13)

Notes

Loved By God

1. For God so loves me that He gave His only Son to die for me. (John 3:16)
2. I am fully and unconditionally loved by God, and there is nothing I could do or not do to change that.
3. Nothing can separate me from God's love. (Romans 8:38-39)
4. God rejoices over me with singing. (Zephaniah 3:17)
5. God's love is continually pouring into my heart from the Holy Spirit. (Romans 5:5)
6. I am the target of Father God's affection and delight.
7. I have great joy because I am loved and forgiven by God.
8. I delight myself in the Lord and His love for me.
9. I am increasingly and profoundly experiencing God's love for me.
10. I am fully accepted in Jesus.
11. God is a good God with good intentions towards me.
12. God is extravagant in His love towards me.
13. My experience with God's perfect love drives all fear from my life. (1 John 4:18)
14. There is no end to the affection that God has for me.
15. I come to Father God confidently, knowing how much I am loved.

Notes

_____
_____
_____
_____
_____
_____
_____
_____
_____

Freedom From Fear of Rejection

1. I have the spirit of power, love, and a sound mind. (2 Timothy 1:7)
2. I am completely loved and valued by Father God.
3. Father God's perspective is my only consideration in determining my value.
4. People are drawn to me because I have divine favor on my life.
5. I don't shrink back in uncomfortable situations.
6. I am powerful and I determine the response I have towards others.
7. There is no connection between people's opinions of me and my self-worth.
8. I do not react out of fear but always respond out of love.
9. If God wants me to have favor with someone, I will.
10. I am perpetually honest and true to who I am.
11. I don't adjust myself out of fear of not meeting people's expectations.
12. I am free to speak without reservation.
13. I have unshakable confidence.
14. I do not perform for love and acceptance.
15. I do not adjust or change who I am to avoid rejection.

Notes

MY PURPOSE

My Future

1. I am forgetting the negative things in my past and reaching forward to great things in the future. (Philippians 3:13)
2. My future is blessed because of the promises of God.
3. My future is full of limitless potential.
4. In the days and years to come, I will reap the good spiritual seeds I have sown. (Galatians 6:9)
5. I believe the future will be better than the present, and I have the power to help make it so.
6. God knows my future and it is full of hope and peace, not evil. (Jeremiah 29:11)
7. My ultimate purpose in life is to know Jesus and make Him known.
8. I do not worry about the future, but I radically trust God's promises about any uncertainties I have.
9. I make good decisions that propel me into my destiny.
10. I have unexpected opportunities coming to me.
11. My positive influence in society is getting stronger each year I love.
12. I do not live in regret or shame, but I anticipate the good coming into my life.
13. Great things are ahead for me in my life.
14. I see my future through the lens of hope.
15. I will be celebrated for how I lived my life.

Having Strong Convictions

1. I have the spirit of power, love, and a sound mind. (2 Timothy 1:7)
2. I am completely loved and valued by Father God.
3. Father God's perspective is my only consideration in determining my value.
4. People are drawn to me because I have divine favor on my life.
5. I don't shrink back in uncomfortable situations.
6. I am powerful and I determine the response I have towards others.
7. There is no connection between people's opinions of me and my self-worth.
8. I do not react out of fear but always respond out of love.
9. If God wants me to have favor with someone, I will.
10. I am perpetually honest and true to who I am.
11. I don't adjust myself out of fear of not meeting people's expectations.
12. I am free to speak without reservation.
13. I have unshakable confidence.
14. I do not perform for love and acceptance.
15. I do not adjust or change who I am to avoid rejection.

Notes

Influence

1. My positive influence increases daily. (2 Corinthians 10:15)
2. My gift makes room for me and brings me before people of influence. (Proverbs 18:16)
3. I consistently bring God encounters to other people. (Mark 16:17-18)
4. My victories create breakthroughs for many others.
5. I am growing in favor with God and man. (Luke 2:52)
6. I positively influence my family, my church, my place of employment, my city, and my nation.
7. I powerfully influence the atmosphere around me.
8. Because I have great hope, I have great influence.
9. People sense God's presence when I talk with them.
10. I am a thermostat that changes the spiritual atmosphere around me.
11. People stop and listen to what I have to say.
12. People move forward in their purpose because of my influence.
13. I am sought after for answers and solutions, and people have a high value for my input.
14. People feel safe under my influence, and I am trusted by many.
15. I am recognized as a leader with or without a position or title of influence.

Notes

SPIRITUAL PRACTICES

Reading The Bible

1. I I love to read the Bible! I expect to encounter God and receive revelations from what I read today that will change my life.
2. God's word does not depart from my mouth, and I meditate on it day and night so that I will make my way prosper and have good success. (Joshua 1:8)
3. I am a doer of the word not just a hearer. (James 1:22)
4. Revelation comes to me when I read the Word.
5. The Word is living and active in me.
6. I consistently make time every day to read my Bible.
7. When I read the Word, lies I have believed are exposed and displaced with the truth.
8. The Holy Spirit leads me in my interpretation of the Bible.
9. There is nothing I am facing that Scripture cannot speak into.
10. I have strong motivation and spiritual hunger to spend time in the Bible.
11. Every aspect of my life is impacted through the time I spend meditating on Scripture.
12. It is easy for me to communicate what I am learning from the Bible.
13 .I claim and receive the promises of Scripture for my life and for my descendants.
14. My life inspires multitudes to love the Bible, understand the Bible, and be transformed by the Bible.
15. I encounter God's love and power every time I am in His Word.

Powerful Prayers

1. My prayers are powerful and effective. (James 5:16)
2. My faith is being strengthened to possess all that Jesus won for me. (Romans 4:17-23)
3. I pray without ceasing for this is the will of God. (1 Thessalonians 5:17-18)
4. I call out to God and He answers me and He shows me great and mighty things which I do not yet know. (Jeremiah 33:3)
5. I'm fully convinced that God will do what He has promised. (Romans 4:21)
6. Whatever I ask for in Jesus' name is done for me. (John 14:13)
7. I am confident that God hears me when I approach him and ask according to His will. (1 John 5:14)
8. I know that because God hears me, I have what I ask for. (1 John 5:15)
9. I come boldly to God with my needs because of His grace. (Hebrews 4:16)
10. My powerful beliefs and prayers are dislodging demonic activity in my region.
11. I am a person of continual prayer and gratitude.
12. I have faith in seemingly impossible situations.
13. I have faith in the unseen realm.
14. Every time I pray, something happens whether I "feel it" or not.
15. My prayers change the course of nations and generations.

Notes

_____

_____

_____

_____

_____

_____

SPIRITUAL PRACTICES

Thankfulness

1. I am known by God and people as an incredibly thankful person.
2. I am thankful for every good thing in my life, and even thankful for the challenges that are strengthening me.
3. I give thanks in every circumstance, for this is the will of God. (1 Thessalonians 5:18)
4. I am not anxious about anything but overcome anxiety with thankfulness. (Philippians 4:6-7)
5. I give thanks to the Lord with all my heart and tell of all His wonderful deeds. (Psalm 9:1)
6. I love bringing glory to God by being thankful. (2 Corinthians 4:15)
7. I give thanks to the Lord for his unfailing love and his wonderful deeds. (Psalm 107:8)
8. I find things to be thankful for even when I don't feel like it. (Psalm 50:14)
9. I continually give thanks for all that has been given to me through Jesus. (2 Corinthians 9:15)
10. I overflow with gratitude. (Colossians 2:7)
11. My thanksgiving positions me to trust God.
12. Being thankful is a lifestyle for me.
13. My gratitude shifts the atmosphere around me.
14. I enter into God's presence with thanksgiving. (Psalm 100:4)
15. My continual victory in Jesus causes me to be thankful. (1 Corinthians 15:57)

Notes

_____
_____
_____
_____
_____

Evangelism Part 1

1. The love of Christ compels me to share with people what is on God's heart for them. (2 Corinthians 5:14)
2. I share what is on God's heart fearlessly because I am motivated by love and love casts out all fear. (1 John 4:18)
3. I am not ashamed of the gospel for it is the power of God for salvation for everyone who believes. (Romans 1:16)
4. I have a powerful evangelistic anointing, and I love telling people about Jesus.
5. My personality or past doesn't disqualify me from sharing the gospel effectively.
6. Everyone is searching for the Good News that I have!
7. I am comfortable in talking to strangers about spiritual matters.
8. Jesus loves non-believers, especially atheists.
9. God always shows up when people mock or ridicule me because of my faith.
10. I am a bold witness of Christ's resurrection power.
11. God confirms His Word with signs and wonders when I share my faith.
12. Everywhere I go, I am overwhelmed by the love of God for people, and I am highly motivated to share the gospel.
13. It is easy and normal for me to articulate the gospel.
14. I have a unique way to evangelize.
15. Today my mind and spirit will tune into the people around me and find those who desire to be saved. I will lead those people to Jesus.

Notes

_____

_____

_____

_____

_____

Evangelism Part 2

1. I am fearless, courageous, and I live with an understanding that people are hungry for Jesus.
2. I am creative in my evangelism, and I adapt well to bring powerful God-encounters to different kinds of people.
3. My family respects me and wants to hear from me because my Christian life is very attractive to them. It is easy to share the gospel with them because they want to know the God that is inside of me.
4. My reputation for leading people to Jesus is so widely known in my town that when people want to get saved, they find me.
5. When I feel afraid to share the gospel with someone, I remind myself that on the other side of fear is a testimony.
6. I consistently lead people into a relationship with Jesus.
7. God is using my past and life experiences to help me connect with and share God's love with those who need to encounter Jesus.
8. Every evangelistic seed I plant and every seed I water will bear fruit.
9. When I hear the word evangelism or evangelist, I get excited.
10. I positively influence those who are called into the office of the evangelist.
11. I have a great passion to see people spend eternity in heaven, not hell.
12. I am not intimidated to share the goodness of God with any type of person.
13. I have great influence in the lives of those "least likely" to be saved.
14. I am inspired by the passion of other evangelists, and I ignite a fire in others as well.
15. When I share Jesus, people do not feel condemnation or but feel overwhelmed with the Truth and Love of Jesus Christ.

Notes

_____

_____

_____

WORSHIP

My Worship

1. I am a true worshipper and worship God in spirit and in truth. (John 4:8)
2. I rejoice in the Lord always, for this is the will of God. (1 Thessalonians 5:16,18)
3. I am always thankful which brings me into His presence. (Psalm 100:4)
4. Because God's love for me is better than life, my mouth glorifies Him. (Psalm 63:3)
5. I am known in heaven as a man after God's own heart.
6. I am going to new levels of passion in my worship.
7. I joyfully celebrate Jesus. I love to worship God!
8. I am always discovering new aspects of God's nature that leads to greater worship.
9. I feel connected to God in my worship.
10. I get excited when I don't feel like worshiping because it is an opportunity to give a sacrifice of praise and adoration.
11. As I worship, I acquire heaven's perspective over my life and situation, and I start seeing things as He sees them.
12. When I worship, Jesus is glorified, heaven invades earth, and hell shakes in terror.
13. I am drawn to the presence of God.
14. Worship for me is a lifestyle, not an event.
15. I worship God no matter what circumstances look like in my life.

Worship Leading

1. My praise flows from the knowledge that I am loved by the Father and do not have to earn it.
2. I step into supernatural giftings, skills, and anointings when playing instruments and leading worship.
3. I hear the songs of heaven and catch the wind of the Spirit in corporate settings.
4. My voice and songs release supernatural healing and deliverance.
5. When I lead worship, I inspire others to bring their full hearts before the Lord.
6. My passion to worship God is contagious.
7. My worship fights battles I never knew about and destroys the plans of the enemy while my focus is on my Father.
8. Every time I worship, I step into deep intimacy and high praise.
9. When I lead worship, I take people into deeper encounters and higher places than they've ever seen before.
10. Musical ability comes naturally to me.
11. Like David, I am a person pursuing and running after God's own heart.
12. I have an unusual ability to have healthy relationships with church leaders and those who are leading church services. I seek first to understand them before I seek to be understood by them.
13. I am skilled in creating and maintaining healthy relationships of the teams I am leading.
14. I easily build trust with people because of my integrity, honoring of people, and the presence of God released through me.

Notes

Leading a Team

1. I have an unusual ability to inspire people.
2. I am proactive in my thinking and planning, thus my team members can trust me.
3. My team members are excited about coming to a worship practice led by me.
4. I build great people, not just good worship team members or musicians.
5. The Holy Spirit is obviously leading our worship team.
6. I can help every person on my team to go higher in their musical ability and in their heart for worship.
7. I am a clear communicator and have good conflict resolution skills.
8. I can be influenced by my team, but I am not a people pleaser.
9. I give revelation to my team about the power of honoring the leaders who are overseeing our ministry.
10. The ministry teams I lead have people of high character and who radically love Jesus.
11. I worship the Lord with all my heart whether I'm alone or with a team.
12. I love coming under the vision of church leaders and service leaders.
13. There is no personality type that I don't connect with.
14. I make lifelong connections with my worship teams.
15. I feel the pleasure of God when I lead worship with a team.

Notes

Spontaneous Worship

1. There is always a new song to the Lord rising up in my heart.
2. I am created to be connected to the Spirit.
3. It is easy for me to sing/play outside the structure of a worship set.
4. I flow with the Spirit because I trust Him more than I trust our plans.
5. I have a great, natural awareness of time and am always conscientious of what the Lord is doing in a room, not just in me.
6. It is just as natural for me to sing/play spontaneously as it is for me to follow the set list.
7. I am always in tune with the Lord's heart for a room and a worship set.
8. I love coming under my leaders and it is easy for me to trust what they feel.
9. I am adaptable and am filled with exhilaration when we abandon our plans to follow the Spirit.
10. I understand the heart of my leaders concerning their philosophy about the role of spontaneous worship.
11. I am always aware of the angelic moving in a room, and see the spirit realm affected when our team flows with the Presence.
12. My leaders trust me, and I trust myself to follow what I hear the Lord doing.
13. I love listening to the song of the Lord, and it's so natural for me to sing/play it too.
14. I feel the Lord's pleasure pouring over me when I sing from my heart and spirit.
15. I am not worried about making mistakes or singing/playing perfectly because I am not performing for love but am lifting my song from the place of being fully adored.

Notes

_____

_____

_____

RELATIONSHIPS

Walking in Love

1. I love the Lord my God with all my heart, with all my soul, with all my strength, and with all my mind. And I love my neighbor as myself. (Luke 10:27)
2. God's love is perfected in me. (1 John 4:12)
3. I regard people through prophetic eyes and not according to the flesh. (2 Corinthians 5:16)
4. Love never fails. (1 Corinthians 13:8)
5. In everything I do, I pursue love.
6. I see the good in others and call that out of them.
7. People's behaviors do not determine my level of love for them.
8. I am moved with compassion towards people.
9. I think the best of people and give them the benefit of the doubt.
10. I am happy when others to succeed and I cheer them on.
11. I release security in the atmosphere and people feel safe with me.
12. I am a good listener.
13. I enjoy people and I am comfortable to be myself with them.
14. I refuse to gossip about other people but only speak well of others.
15. I have great wisdom in knowing when to set boundaries that establish what I can and cannot do in loving others.

Difficult Relationships

1. I am in control of me and no one else is responsible for my internal peace and joy. (Galatians 5:22-23, 2 Timothy 1:7)
2. When I have relational difficulty with someone, I only talk to them and those who are part of the solution. (Matthew 18:15)
3. Every day I am receiving greater compassion for those I've had difficulty with.
4. In relationships I first seek to understand before seeking to be understood.
5. I ask good questions and avoid making assumptions about other people.
6. I am a great communicator in relationships.
7. It is easy for me to see the gold inside of people I have difficulty with.
8. I don't need to agree with everyone to thrive in life.
9. I carry the gift of reconciliation.
10. I know how to set healthy boundaries with people.
11. My love for difficult people changes the atmosphere of my relationships.
12. I know when to speak and when to listen.
13. I have access to God's unlimited wisdom that brings solutions to evert challenging relationship.
14. I am only moved by love and not by anger or fear in difficult relationships.
15. I am not afraid of brave communication, and boldly protect connection in my relationships.

Notes

_____
_____
_____
_____

Conflict Resolution

1. I am exceptional at resolving conflict in a healthy, loving way that empowers others and restores relationships.
2. When I have a difficulty with someone, I talk to them and not others about it. (Matthew 18:15)
3. I am not afraid of tense discussions or conflict because I have a strong ability to communicate challenging things with grace and these conversations always bring unity.
4. I always know what to do when there is a relationship challenge in my life.
5. I don't jump to conclusions or make assumptions about other people's motives.
6. I know when to pursue a matter and when to let things go.
7. I always seek to understand other people's hearts before addressing issues with them.
8. I genuinely believe the best about the people in my life.
9. I joyfully embrace opportunities to resolve conflict with others.
10. My value for healthy communication and conflict resolution has set a positive example to my friends, family, and colleagues of what good relationships look like.
11. I value relationship above the pain or inconvenience of confrontation and am passionate about wholehearted connection.
12. When others seek to resolve conflict with me, I am open, receptive, and willing to make necessary changes in my life.
13. My love for people covers a multitude of sins (and disagreements).
14. I am not afraid of being honest with my heart.
15. I quickly resolve conflicts and the sun doesn't go down on my anger.

Notes

RELATIONSHIPS

Unbelievers (Part 1)

1. God desires all people to be saved. (1 Timothy 2:4, 2 Peter 3:9)
2. _____ is convinced that God exists.
3. _____ is convinced that God is inherently good.
4. _____ is ripe for an encounter with Father God.
5. _____ knows the immeasurable love of God.
6. _____ is being led to repentance by the kindness of God.
7. _____ is actively being pursued by Holy Spirit!
8. _____ knows the truth and the truth sets him/her free.
9. _____ 's spirit receives revelation from Holy Spirit.
10. _____ has encounters with the Holy Spirit when he/she sleeps.
11. _____ pursues relationship with God.
12. _____ 's heart is open to receiving the gospel.
13. _____ is drawn to intimacy with God.
14. _____ has divine and angelic encounters.
15. _____ is free from all spiritual bondage.

Notes

_____
_____
_____
_____
_____
_____
_____
_____
_____
_____
_____
_____

Unbelievers (Part 2)

1. _____ has regular divine appointments with life-giving believers.
2. _____'s heart is soft and open to the Holy Spirit's work in him/her/them.
3. _____ will not perish but will come to repentance.
4. _____ is becoming aware of the conviction of the Holy Spirit.
5. _____ will confess that Jesus is the Lord of their life.
6. _____ will call on the name of the Lord and is saved.
7. _____'s curiosity for God and the supernatural is growing every day.
8. _____ Holy Spirit is reminding _____ of encounters with the Father from their childhood.
9. Jesus is fully redeeming ___'s experience with Christians and the Church.
10. _____ is receiving a supernatural grace to forgive and let go.
11. I am a consistent powerful and positive influence in _____'s life.
12. The Father is relentless in His pursuit of _____, and is opening his/her eyes to see it.
13. Negative spiritual influence is losing its authority over ___.
14. _____ will see the goodness of God in the land of the living!
15. _____ will be a strong believer radically influencing many for Jesus.

Notes

_____

_____

_____

_____

_____

_____

The Words I Speak

1. I am a powerful and influential communicator.
2. I set the course of my life with my words. (James 3:2-5)
3. The words of my mouth and the meditation of my heart are acceptable in God's sight. (Psalm 19:14)
4. I am releasing life through the power of my tongue. (Proverbs 18:21)
5. I am slow to speak and quick to listen. (James 1:19)
6. I speak pleasant words that are sweet to the soul and healing to the bones. (Proverbs 16:24).
7. I speak words of wisdom that bring healing. (Proverbs 12:18)
8. I communicate in love and truth simultaneously. (Ephesians 4:15)
9. My words are filled with wisdom and hope.
10. I inspire people when I speak.
11. My words carry authority and are anointed.
12. I am known as a great encourager.
13. I am careful with my words and refuse to gossip about others.
14. I am very successful in the conversations I have with a wide variety of people.
15. I build up the people in my life with my words.

Notes

Patience

1. I am a truly patient person and my patience levels are increasing daily.
2. My hope for what I don't see yet causes me to be patient. (Romans 8:25)
3. I don't quit doing the right things because I know it will pay off eventually. (Galatians 6:9)
4. I don't get frustrated when I have to wait longer for answers than others around me. (Psalm 37:7-9)
5. My love for people is expressed in my patience towards them. (1 Corinthians 13:4)
6. As I wait on the Lord, my strength is being renewed.
7. I am strengthened with all power, according to God's glorious might, so I can have great endurance and patience. (Colossians 1:11)
8. The Spirit is continually producing the fruit of patience in me. (Galatians 5:22)
9. I handle delays with extreme joyfulness.
10. My hope level doesn't drop when things don't turn out as planned.
11. I live at a high level of inner contentment.
12. When others give up on people or promises, I keep going.
13. Challenges only strengthen my resolve and perseverance.
14. I fully trust God for the timing of things.
15. I have a high tolerance for difficult people and situations.

Notes

_____
_____
_____
_____
_____
_____

FAMILY RELATIONSHIPS

Future Spouse (Part 1)

1. I am trusting in the Lord, and He will give me the desires of my heart. (Psalm 37:4)
2. God has great marriage plans for me and my future spouse.
3. I am fully content as a single person but look forward with hopeful expectation towards the good that is coming through a godly, deeply-loving marriage.
4. I am at peace about finding someone to marry.
5. I am thankful for what God is doing in me as I am waiting.
6. I do not let the fear of disappointment prevent me from being open to relationships.
7. I am a person who is easily able to give and receive love.
8. I am willing to open my heart to move towards connection.
9. I am open to building a life-long relationship with someone.
10. I do not let past relationships or failures shape my beliefs about future opportunities.
11. I do not settle for a relationship with someone just to fill an emotional void in me.
12. I wait patiently for my spouse, full of hope for a great future with them.
13. I attract healthy people who know how to build intimate relationships.
14. I am the kind of person that would be great to marry.
15. I am able to stay in contentment and avoid desperation.

Future Spouse (Part 2)

1. My spouse and I will enter into relationship with wholeness in our hearts.
2. My spouse and I will be equally yoked in passion and purpose.
3. My spouse is growing into the person I will enjoy being married to.
4. My spouse is passionate for God and His word.
5. My spouse is a person of purity, high integrity, and character.
6. The union I will have with my spouse will please God.
7. The story my spouse and I have will inspire other single people to wait for the marriage God has for them.
8. My spouse is designed to be attracted to me, and I don't have to work to get their attention.
9. I am perfectly placed in the center of God's plan for my marriage.
10. My spouse and I will have a unique ability to communicate and protect our connection.
11. My excitement for my future marriage is balanced with peace and trust in the Lord's plan.
12. There is nothing wrong with me! I'm waiting because my Father has good plans for me. (Jeremiah 29:11)
13. I am desirable, attractive, mature, intelligent, confident, lovable, and ready for marriage.
14. God is making me into someone who will love and serve my future spouse in the way they deserve.
15. My spouse and I will leave a legacy of connection, passion, unity, courage, and a long-lasting, joyful marriage that will inspire others for generations.

Notes

_____

_____

_____

_____

_____

FAMILY RELATIONSHIPS

My Marriage (Part 1)

1. Wives: As a wife, I submit myself to my husband as is fitting in the Lord. My husband loves me like Christ loved the church and gave Himself up for her. Husbands: As a husband, I love my wife as Christ loved the church and gave Himself up for her. (Colossians 3:18-19, Ephesians 5:22-26)
2. Wives: The heart of my husband trusts in me. He has no lack of gain.
   Husbands: I express belief in my wife and encourage her. She has no lack of gain. (Proverbs 31:11, 28-29)
3. Wives: I do my husband good and not evil all the days of my life. (Proverbs 31:12)
   Husbands: I cover my wife with the Word to present her holy and blameless before the Lord. (Ephesians 5:26)
4. My spouse and I have a unity and intimacy found in the Trinity.
5. My spouse and I continually grow in deeper hunger for God.
6. I have a satisfying and fulfilling marriage with _____ .
7. I recognize _____ as a gift from God to my life.
8. I show honor to _____ with my family, friends and coworkers.
9. I am able to easily see the gold inside of _____ .
10. I give _____ grace to not be perfect, and I always celebrate his or her progress.
11. I give _____ the benefit of the doubt when issues arise.
12. _____ and I finish disagreements, and we don't let the sun go down on our anger.
13. I do not hold grudges against _____ but quickly work through offenses with him/her.
14. I refuse to have any unspoken expectations on _____ .
15. I value what _____ contributes to my life.

Notes

_____

_____

_____

DECLARE IT

My Marriage (Part 2)

1. I work to help _____ be the best version of himself/herself.
2. God always shows up when I think _____ is not meeting my needs.
3. I understand _____'s legitimate needs, and I am growing in meeting those needs.
4. _____ and I work together in unity and strength.
5. _____ and I share honestly without any hiddenness.
6. _____ and I bravely communicate while protecting our connection with one another.
7. _____ and I value laughter in our relationship.
8. I am able to show _____ love in ways he/she understands.
9. My love for _____ is always increasing.
10. I only have eyes for my spouse.
11. Our best days are ahead of us.
12. I am physically, emotionally, and spiritually attracted to my spouse more than I could have dreamed.
13. I feel the overwhelming pleasure and affection of the Lord when I go out of my way to love and serve my spouse.
14. My marriage is bringing glory to God every day, and inspires the marriages of others.
15. The love and connection my spouse and I have for each other is restoring disappointments and pain other people have towards marriage.

Notes

_____

_____

_____

_____

_____

_____

FAMILY RELATIONSHIPS

Children / Parenting (Part 1)

1. My prayers are powerful and effective for my family members.
2. It is easy to teach my kids the ways and principles of the Kingdom.
3. I have an abundance of solutions and wisdom for every situation my family encounters.
4. My children feel safe, free, and loved in our home.
5. I am raising up powerful world-changers in my home.
6. I know how to discipline and empower my kids in ways that produce health and life.
7. My children are secure because they know how much God and I love them.
8. It is easy for me to have open and honest conversations with my children.
9. My children and I encounter God together.
10. I do not overly protect my children from the consequences of their wrong choices.
11. I easily apologize to my children and ask their forgiveness when I have wronged them.
12. My children have great grace on them to make healthy choices concerning relationships, social media, finances, life habits, and their sexuality.
13. My kids feel safe to tell me anything, and I always know how to respond to what they share.
14. I am not afraid of decisions my kids will make because I trust the Lord to lead them like He has lead me.
15. I am engaged, attentive, and present with my family.

Notes

_____

_____

_____

_____

Children / Parenting (Part 2)

1. My children are a gift from the Lord. (Psalm 127:3)
2. Each of my family members has favor and radically loves Jesus. (Acts 16:30-31)
3. The Lord is building our house and a legacy for our family. (Psalms 127:1)
4. I create strongholds of blessing in my family.
5. God is faithful to heal the relationships in my family.
6. My children have wisdom, love, prosperity, and peace in every area of their lives.
7. I am a great parent and my family is joyful!
8. All of my children are free from generational curses and are accessing all the generational blessings from their ancestors.
9. My children are great friends with one another and genuinely enjoy each other's company.
10. My spouse and I are in unity about how to raise our children and always lead them into a deeper, personal connection with God.
11. I am a consistent parent.
12. I respond with love and wisdom to whatever my child does.
13. I have wealth and property to pass on to my children's children.
14. I follow through on what I tell my children I will do.
15. I understand the differences in my children, and I have insight into how to love, inspire, and direct each of them according to who they are.

Notes

_____

_____

_____

_____

_____

Parenting Grown Children

1. I have great hope for every member of my family.
2. The best seasons of my family life are ahead.
3. I have great favor in the eyes of my adult children and their families.
4. God is completely committed to all of my family relationships, and He is at work doing more than I see.
5. I make good decisions concerning how much to help my adult children.
6. I see the unique design of my children and value their uniqueness.
7. My grandchildren are blessed, protected, influential, wise, and lovers of Jesus.
8. I get along incredibly well with my children'as' spouses and their families.
9. There is new grace on my relationship with my adult children for us to be closer than ever.
10. I can thrive personally and spiritually even if my children are not making good decisions.
11. God is mightily strengthening the churches where my children live.
12. I know what to say and not to say in my relationships with my adult children.
13. My prayers for my adult children are working, and I am in a new season of effective praying and believing for my family.
14. Family holidays are full of peace, and are getting better each year.
15. I do not enable or control my children.

Notes

DECLARE IT

Relationships with My Parents

1. Because I honor my parents, things go well for me and I live a long life. (Ephesians 6:3)
2. My parents are having life-changing encounter with God's love and power.
3. I forgive my parents for any hurt or pain they have caused in my life.
4. I have a healthy relationship with my parents.
5. I am being drawn into a deeper relationship with my parents.
6. My prayers for my parents are working.
7. I am a powerful influencer in the lives of my parents.
8. I am full of hope for the future of my family.
9. The Lord loves to reunite estranged families and he is currently working on any disconnection or distance in my family.
10. When I think about my parents, I am full of peace and gratefulness.
11. I know how to relate to my parents at any age.
12. I see when my parents are pursuing and caring for me, and we are great at communicating love to each other.
13. God is a father to the fatherless, and loves to step in where my parents can't.
14. My parents and I are closer than we have ever been, and have an unusual grace to forgive and understand each other.
15. I am receiving an inheritance of covering and blessings from my parents every day.

Notes

_____
_____
_____
_____
_____
_____

Spiritual Parents

1. I am a magnet for healthy, intentional spiritual parents.
2. I am naturally vulnerable and wholehearted, and I love being accountable to leaders in my life to see blind spots and bring healthy correction.
3. The Lord satisfies all my desires with good things, and he cares about my desire to have spiritual parents.
4. My leaders and I have an unusual gift to communicate expectations well, and we always navigate towards connection when we are feeling disappointment.
5. Wanting spiritual parents is a healthy, biblical need. God always helps me find balance in my desires.
6. I am confident in going to the Lord first for my fathering needs because He is always the perfect Father to me. (Matthew 6:33)
7. I am loved beyond measure, and the Lord's overwhelming love for me attracts leaders who want to lead and love me well.
8. I am secure in who I am, and do not doubt my identity as a son/daughter even when it seems I do not have any fathers/mothers around me.
9. It is God's heart to surround me with family.
10. God's grace always shows up for me when I am feeling awkward, needy, or insecure around leaders.
11. God is surrounding me with pure, healthy, intentional, noble, protective fathers.
12. God is surrounding me with strong, compassionate, insightful, nurturing, loving, prophetic mothers.
13. I don't just receive from spiritual parents, but am a great strength in their lives helping move forward the callings and dreams they have.
14. I am not looking for one person to meet all my spiritual parenting needs, but I have healthy expectations of what each can and cannot do for me.
15. I am increasingly becoming a strong spiritual parent to others.

DECLARE IT
Pregnancy

1. Any negative postpartum symptoms can not come near me or my family.
2. I am covered, and so surrounded by people who adore our family.
3. My body is thriving while I am pregnant and will continue to thrive after I give birth.
4. My whole family walks in supernatural protection and covering - the enemy cannot get near us!
5. I will carry my baby to full term with no complications.
6. My baby is developing at the perfect rate and has everything he/she needs to grow and thrive.
7. My body was designed by God to carry this baby, therefore my body will grow and stretch, as needed, without injury, trauma, or scarring.
8. I will not fear anything concerning this pregnancy, or the health, life, and peace of my child. (2 Timothy 1:7)
9. Thank you, Jesus, for giving me your peace! I daily live the abundance of peace. (John 14:27)
10. Father, you have made me a joyful mother of children and I live daily in overflowing joy! (Psalm 113:9)
11. I daily gain strength during and after this pregnancy for the joy of the Lord is my strength! (Nehemiah 8:10)
12. Lord, you have given me the grace, anointing, and wisdom to be the mother/father of my child!
13. I am lacking nothing, my child will live a blessed life full of love, provision, favor, and peace.
14. I will not labor in vain or have trouble delivering my child for we are both blessed by the Lord. (Isaiah 65:23)
15. I thank you, Father, for your promise of taking sickness out of my midst. (Exodus 23:25)
    Therefore I will have a happy, healthy pregnancy with no negative sicknesses or diseases.

PHYSICAL BODY

Healthy Body

1. I love to exercise, eat right, drink a lot of water, and laugh.
2. My body is healthy, whole, brimming with energy, pain-free, and getting stronger everyday.
3. My body is the temple of the Holy Spirit, and He is empowering me with bodily health now. (1 Corinthians 6:19)
4. I glorify God with what I do with my body. (1 Corinthians 6:20)
5. I am fearfully and wonderfully made. (Psalm 139:14)
6. I laugh easily and often, and I find joy in everyday life knowing that it brings health and life to my body. (Proverbs 17:22)
7. I love and celebrate the body that God gave to me.
8. I crave healthy foods and appropriate proportions.
9. It is easy for me to maintain a healthy weight for my body and live a consistent, healthy lifestyle.
10. I eat to feed the needs of my body rather than the needs of my soul, and I consistently make good choices with the food I eat.
11. My body gets to enjoy the Presence of Holy Spirit who lives in me.
12. My body is a fat-burning machine.
13. I love exercising and it is easy for me to prioritize exercise into my daily schedule.
14. I support and love my body instead of hating and working against it.
15. My healthiest days are ahead of me.

Healing

1. I have life in every cell of my body because the Spirit that raised Christ from the dead lives in me. (Romans 8:11)
2. By His stripes, I have already been healed. (Isaiah 53:5).
3. Today, divine solutions and miracles are being released for my total healing.
4. God always shows up when I get a bad doctor's report.
5. My faith is not dependent upon what I see, feel, or experience, but it is dependent on God's Word.
6. I get healed and release healing more easily than anyone I know.
7. There is nothing separating me from the healing grace of Jesus.
8. I am a magnet for healing, and people around me constantly get healed.
9. I am worthy to walk in divine health through the blood of Jesus.
10. It is extremely easy for people in my region of the world to get healed.
11. I am immune to sickness and disease because I am a new creation with new DNA.
12. My family and I are free from generational illnesses through a divine swap of our inheritance for Jesus' inheritance.
13. I am living in ever-increasing health. My eyes, bones, hearing, central nervous system, organs, and muscles get stronger and stronger the longer I live.
14. My immune system grows stronger every day.
15. My healthiest days are ahead of me.

Notes

PHYSICAL BODY

Sleep

1. I sleep in peace because Father God keeps me safe. (Psalm 4:8)
2. Whenever I sleep, my sleep is sweet. (Proverbs 3:24)
3. My mind moves towards Father God as I am falling asleep. (Isaiah 26:3)
4. I am able to sleep well even when there are challenging circumstances. (Luke 8:23)
5. I am able to sleep without anxiety because God's grace is available for what I will face tomorrow. (Matthew 6:34)
6. The peace of God guards my heart and my mind even while I'm sleeping. (Philippians 4:6-7)
7. I fall asleep easily and without effort.
8. I have supernatural dreams while sleeping which have great influence on others and me.
9. I get the right amount of sleep for my body.
10. God's angels protect me while I sleep.
11. All my loved ones also sleep well and are free from nightmares and night terrors.
12. I encounter the presence of God while I sleep.
13. My spirit is active and receives affirmation, insight, and answers from Holy Spirit while I sleep.
14. I wake up in peace, and fully rested and refreshed.
15. I am renewed, body, soul, and spirit during my sleep.

Notes

_____
_____
_____
_____
_____
_____

DECLARE IT

Weight Loss

1. My body is the temple of the Holy Spirit. (1 Corinthians 6:19)
2. I am supernaturally empowered with self-control by the Holy Spirit. (Galatians 5:22-23)
3. Whether I eat or drink, I do all to the glory of God. (1 Corinthians 10:31)
4. I am prospering and in health even as my soul is prospering. (3 John 2)
5. Today, I am receiving keys and long-term solutions from God for the best ways for me to lose weight.
6. The scale doesn't determine my value.
7. I am fearfully and wonderfully made, and I find my identity in how God sees me. (Psalm 139)
8. I consistently live at a healthy weight for my body type.
9. I crave healthy food.
10. I am motivated to lose weight and become healthy.
11. I find it easy to lose weight in a healthy way.
12. I am a fat-burning machine.
13. I enjoy exercising and discover new ways to exercise that I love on a regular basis.
14. I have the ability to lose weight and keep it off.
15. I set a good example for my family by living a healthy lifestyle and caring for my body in a loving, compassionate way.

Notes

_____
_____
_____
_____
_____
_____
_____

Energy

1. I wait on the Lord and He renews my strength. (Isaiah 40:31)
2. My youthful energy is renewed like eagles. (Psalm 103:5)
3. I have a sufficient supply of grace from God. (2 Corinthians 2:9)
4. God's strength is made perfect in my weakness, so when I am weak, then I am strong. (2 Corinthians 12:9-10)
5. My body is receiving supernatural strength because the Spirit that raised Jesus from the dead lives in me. (Romans 8:11)
6. Today, I can do all things through Christ who strengthens me. (Philippians 4:13)
7. God gives me strength when I'm weary and increases my power. (Isaiah 40:29)
8. Today, I am strong in the Lord and in His mighty power. (Ephesians 6:10)
9. I have abounding energy like children!
10. Because I am in His presence, I feel refreshed and full of His life and power.
11. When I'm tired, God surprises me with supernatural energy and brings the perfect people my way to help me.
12. Even though I feel weak at times, I am really strong.
13. God has an unending supply of strength for me today.
14. I always catch a second wind when I start to feel tired.
15. I will outlast every challenge and overcome every obstacle today.

Notes

FINANCES

Mindset of Abundance

1. I honor the Lord with my wealth. (Proverbs 3:9-10)
2. My abundance causes blessing and well-being for multitudes.
3. The Lord is my Shepherd, and I will not live in lack. (Psalm 23:1)
4. Whatever I do prospers. (Psalm 1:3)
5. I am incredibly overcoming poverty mindsets which restrict my influence and ability to bless people.
6. As a good Father, God wants me to be blessed and enjoy my life.
7. The blessing of the Lord makes me rich, and he adds no sorrow with it. (Proverbs 10:22)
8. God is supplying every need of mine according to His riches in glory in Christ Jesus. (Philippians 4:19)
9. I bring the whole tithe into the storehouse, so that there may be food in Father's house, and He has opened for me the windows of heaven and pours out for me a blessing until it overflows. (Malachi 3:10)
10. God has given me the ability to produce wealth. (Deuteronomy 8:18)
11. I am not anxious about my life, what I will eat or drink, nor about my body, what I will wear. (Matthew 6:25)
12. Because I am seeking first the Kingdom of God and his righteousness, ALL things that I need are being added to me. (Matthew 6:33)
13. I lack no good thing because I seek the Lord! (Psalm 34:10)

FINANCES

14. In all things, at all times, I have all that I need. (2 Corinthians 9:8)
15. I am abundantly blessed in every area of my life.

Notes

Financial Abundance

1. I always have more than enough.
2. I have divine ideas that generate wealth.
3. God richly supplies all my financial needs. (Philippians 4:19)
4. I attract favor, blessing, and wealth.
5. I make great financial decisions.
6. God desires for me to prosper financially.
7. Because I sow finances liberally, I reap abundant finances in my life. (2 Corinthians 9:6)
8. I am an intelligent and wise investor.
9. I receive raises, bonuses, benefits, sales, commissions, favorable settlements, estates, inheritances, interest, income, rebates, returns, checks in the mail, gifts, and surprises.
10. My expenses are decreasing and I walk in continual blessing and increase.
11. I have more than enough to give into the Kingdom of God.
12. I am trustworthy with money. God trusts me with His resources.
13. The distribution of my wealth becomes the answer to the prayers of those in need
14. The wealth that I accrue in my life will be a blessing to my children's children's children.
15. I help others get breakthrough in their finances.

Notes

Generosity

1. I am always receiving seed from God to sow. (2 Corinthians 9:10)
2. I am generous on every occasion. (2 Corinthians 9:11)
3. My giving is love-driven, not guilt-driven.
4. I am a joyful giver and do not give out of obligation.
5. I know when to give, how much to give, and when I am not to give.
6. I am generous to the poor.
7. I overflow with delight as I generously give to the Lord and to others.
8. I am on a generosity rampage, seeking whom I can bless next.
9. I do not worry about lack, knowing God will supply richly all of my needs; therefore, I am able to sow freely and liberally.
10. Because I give, I expect a return that is of good measure, pressed down, shaken together, running over, and pouring out.
11. I give grace generously to myself, and to those in my family. I am generous with my love, patience, and kindness.
12. I have a unique ability to know when God is highlighting someone He is leading me to bless generously with time, money, or another resource.
13. When others are generous towards me, I receive it with gladness.
14. My giving is always increasing.
15. Anyone who gets near me gets blessed.

Notes

_____
_____
_____
_____
_____
_____
_____

Debt

1. I am debt free.
2. Any mountain of debt in my life is being removed from my life. (Mark 11:23)
3. I am living above the world's system of relying on debt. (Matthew 6:33)
4. I am a lender and not a borrower. (Deuteronomy 28:12)
5. I have been redeemed from the curse of debt.
6. I have supernatural debt cancellation operating in my life. (2 Kings 4:1-7)
7. I have an unusual ability to invest and save money.
8. I have an abundance mindset and do not consider lack as part of my life.
9. God is giving me specific wisdom on how to get out of debt.
10. God's riches are currently being released and multiplied financially, spiritually, relationally, and in all areas of my life.
11. I invest extravagantly into the future.
12. As needed, I sacrifice pleasure and nicer things now so I will live debt free in the future.
13. I find supernatural and creative ways to not go into debt.
14. I free others from financial debt.
15. I am full of hope and constantly encouraged when I think about my debt because I know it is getting smaller every day.

Notes

_____

_____

_____

_____

_____

_____

DAILY LIFE

Favor on My Life

1. Favor is a supernatural quality in my life that causes people to like me, to be drawn to me, and it opens doors for me of great influence.
2. Through Jesus, I am 100% loved and worthy to receive all of God's blessings. (Colossians 1:12-14)
3. I find favor and good success in the sight of God and man. (Proverbs 3:4)
4. The Lord gives me favor and honor; He does not withhold good from me. (Psalm 84:11)
5. I am under the blessing of Christ which is a spiritual force working for my good.
6. I am a magnet for unusual favor that impacts those around me.
7. I attract the blessings and favor of God.
8. I carry the substance of favor.
9. I have an anointing that causes others to walk in abundant favor.
10. The favor in my family increases with each new generation.
11. I am constantly stumbling into the favor of God.
12. I have unusual favor with my family, my neighbors ,political leaders, businesses, evangelism, and all areas of my life.
13. I trust myself because the Lord trusts me greatly with the favor He has given me.
14. I am a good steward of the favor on my life, and carry it with wisdom and authority.
15. I use my favor to bless others in great ways.

Today's Favor

1. Life jesus, I am growing in favor with God and man today. (Luke 2:52)
2. My angels are carrying out the Word of God on my behalf. (Psalm 103:20)
3. I serve a mighty God who today will do exceedingly and abundantly beyond all that I can ask or think. (Ephesians 3:20)
4. Favor surrounds me like a shield today. (Psalm 5:12)
5. Today I walk in undeserved favor.
6. A spirit of favor is working on my behalf today in every aspect of my life.
7. I speak to this day, and I call it blessed.
8. I say "God, You are good and I eagerly anticipate Your goodness today."
9. I will succeed in everything I do today.
10. Today, I am positioned for victory.
11. I expect to have divine appointments today, to run into the right people, and to be delivered from the wrong people.
12. God's blessings are manifesting greatly today in my life.
13. My entire family is benefiting from the favor on my life today.
14. I just can't get away from the great benefits of the Lord's favor on me!
15. Today I will use my favor to bless others like never before.

Notes

Decision Making

1. Because I have the mind of Christ and a sound mind, I am a good decision maker. (1 Corinthians 2:16, 2 Timothy 1:7)
2. I will always know what to do. (James 1:5-8)
3. I am not afraid of making wrong choices in my life.
4. I do not make decisions begrudgingly or out of obligation, but I attach faith to every decision I make.
5. I understand delays in hearing God's direction are often a divine setup for me to overcome fear, poverty mindsets, and tendencies in me that have restricted God's ability to lead me into higher things.
6. There is ALWAYS a solution.
7. I understand the times and seasons of my life, and I know what to do. (1 Chronicles 12:32)
8. The decisions I make today are producing blessing for my future generations.
9. I give no place to double-mindedness or regret as I make decisions.
10. I have an excellent process in decision-making that includes Scripture and the wisdom of key people in my life.
11. The seemingly risky decisions I make are based on a clear God-story in my life.
12. I have a great anointing to lead others into the process of good decision-making.
13. I am protected from impulsive, wrong choices in my life.
14. Any bad decisions of the past is now being supernaturally worked out for my good and for God's glory.
15. Like Jesus, when I am making a decision, I look to see what the Father is doing and saying.

Notes

Time Management

1. I am a proactive and intentional person who maximizes my time incredibly.
2. I consistently make time for the most important things of life.
3. I am a punctual person, and it is easy for me to be on time.
4. I accomplish tasks easily and am efficient with time.
5. I meet deadlines with excellence and accuracy.
6. I am a morning person. I wake up on time and start the day in peace.
7. I am not rushed or frantic throughout the day, but I am peaceful and joyful as I fulfill my time commitments.
8. I am able to plan ahead to leave myself plenty of time, even for the unexpected.
9. I am increasingly able to accomplish more in less time.
10. I have divine strategies and ideas for how to manage my time.
11. I honor God with my time and fulfill all His purposes for my life.
12. I walk with an awareness of how I'm investing my time.
13. While making decisions on how to use my time, I think long-term and make decisions that bring me closer to life-long goals.
14. I plan my days well and find scheduling enjoyable and easy.
15. I make sure my family gets the best parts of my time, and I am always present when I'm with them.

Notes

_____
_____
_____
_____
_____
_____

Travel

1. I enjoy traveling, and I am blessed and protected in all my travels.
2. God goes with me and guides me wherever I go. (Psalm 139:7-10)
3. I have an abundance of energy when I travel.
4. I thrive in airports and traffic jams.
5. I quickly recover from long journeys.
6. I sleep well in every place I stay.
7. I easily adapt to wherever I go.
8. I have divine appointments whenever I travel.
9. I have favor with all my flights and connections.
10. Every vehicle I travel in is a protected, safe place.
11. I stay in perfect health when I travel.
12. I have unusual favor with my luggage and belongings always arriving.
13. I regularly receive upgrades and blessings.
14. I do not experience jet lag, but my body quickly adjusts when crossing time zones.
15. Everywhere I go revival breaks out.

Notes

Safety

1. I am blessed, and blessed people are protected. (Deuteronomy 28)
2. I live under supernatural protection. (Psalm 91)
3. All attacks that were headed my way are diverted right now by angelic protection in Jesus' name. (Psalm 91)
4. My angels are carrying out the Word of God on my behalf. (Psalm 103:20)
5. Angels circle around me to protect me. (Psalm 34:7)
6. The Lord makes me dwell in safety. (Psalm 4:8)
7. God covers me and hides me from all harm. (Psalm 17:8)
8. Today, I remain protected inside God, my refuge and shelter. (Psalm 61:3)
9. No weapon intended for me will prevail. (Isaiah 54:17)
10. Every negative word spoken against me will be opposed by God. (Isaiah 54:17)
11. Even when I walk through difficult things, God protects me and is near me. (Psalm 23:4)
12. I feast on God's presence in the midst of my enemies. (Psalm 23:5)
13. God watches over my life and keeps me from all harm. (Psalm 121:7)
14. My life, the lives of my family, and the lives of those close to me are protected from disasters, accidents, false accusation, foolish decisions, and abuse.
15. I live in peace and confidence that I am safe and covered.

Notes

_____
_____
_____
_____
_____
_____

Meetings

1. Every meeting I attend is significant and positively influential.
2. I have an unusual ability to thrive in meetings.
3. My presence in meetings causes great effectiveness and efficiency.
4. I am well-prepared for the meetings I attend or lead.
5. I bring a spirit of unity when I come into meetings.
6. Hope, peace, and joy are released into the room when I speak.
7. I am very articulate when sharing my thoughts.
8. I see important issues that others may miss during discussions.
9. I am a great listener when others are speaking.
10. I am a great discerner in the spirit realm of what is happening in meetings.
11. People feel valued and seen by me in meetings.
12. My words are filled with grace towards everyone in the meeting, even when I am addressing sensitive topics.
13. I honor everyone in the meeting, even when I disagree with their perspective.
14. I am open and honest with my perspectives and share them with respect and humility.
15. My meetings today are going to be the best meetings I've ever been in.

Notes

DECLARE IT

Responsibilities

1. I consistently follow through on what I say I will do. (Matthew 5:37)
2. I am a great steward of what God has given me. (Matthew 25:21)
3. I embrace my responsibilities towards my family, workplace, and to myself with thankfulness, enthusiasm, and joy.
4. Instead of waiting to do something great, I do what is in front of me with great faith.
5. I carry my responsibilities in a place of deep internal rest.
6. I am good at prioritizing my responsibilities.
7. I am able to stay focused on what I need to get done.
8. I complete my responsibilities quickly and with excellence.
9. I keep the "important" tasks in mind and am not overrun by the "urgent" tasks.
10. I set daily goals and complete them.
11. I never feel overwhelmed by what I need to accomplish.
12. I am highly efficient in getting things done.
13. I celebrate my progress, not perfection, towards my goals.
14. I am satisfied with my best, and give my best in everything I do.
15. I am not trying to earn love or approval through my responsible behavior, but I do it from a healthy identity as someone approved by God.

Notes

_____
_____
_____
_____
_____
_____
_____

Job Success

1. Everything I do at my job, I do for the glory of God. (1 Corinthians 10:31)
2. I love making people around me look like geniuses.
3. I love to celebrate people who get promoted ahead of me.
4. I am exceptional at what I do. I am a great blessing to my team, department, and organization.
5. I am developing an incredible skill-set on this job which will benefit this company and me in the future.
6. I have an unusual ability to thrive in diverse work environments.
7. I always know what to do workwise and relationally in my workplace.
8. My presence and ideas create financial increase for my company and ultimately for me.
9. I always find ways to improve the condition of my company.
10. I am a person of high integrity and character.
11. I show up on time and always to do more than what is required of me.
12. I am always growing in my capacity to handle more.
13. I am a joy to those I work with.
14. I receive supernatural insights from Holy Spirit on how to be successful in my job.
15. Just having me on the team brings the favor of God to my workplace.

Notes

MY LEADERSHIP

Empowerment Part. 1
(Inspired by *The Culture of Empowerment*)

1. I'm a radical encourager to everyone around me. (Hebrews 10:25, 1 Thessalonians 5:11)
2. I lead by living a life of integrity. (Ephesians 4:1, Matthew 5:16)
3. The words I speak create a life-giving culture around me. (Proverbs 18:21)
4. Like Jesus, I create a culture of empowerment around me where people thrive.
5. I inspire people, give them opportunities, and I support them in what they do.
6. I inspire people to do what they never thought they could do.
7. I believe in the people I lead more than they believe in themselves.
8. I have an unusual ability to maintain high beliefs about the people in my life.
9. I am full of hope for people.
10. I am full of hope for my own life.
11. I make people feel important and valuable.
12. I identity positive qualities in people and consistently thank them for those.
13. I have a strong sense of loyalty to the people on my team.
14. I care for the whole person and not just what the person can do for me.
15. I am consistent in how I treat and respect people.

Empowerment Part. 2
(Inspired by *The Culture of Empowerment*)

1. I have a "win-win" mindset for everyone on the team.
2. I really see people the way God sees them.
3. I understand the normal patterns of relationships (excitement, disappointment, growth), and I don't withdraw or get afraid when my relationships have moments of disappointment.
4. I believe that a person's negative qualities are usually immature aspects of strengths in their life.
5. When I need to have boundaries in relationships, I do so from a heart of kind firmness, not from anger or frustration.
6. I give others an opportunity to influence me.
7. I pay attention to key things that people say.
8. I regularly use my favor to help open doors for others.
9. I help people get more "wins" in their lives.
10. I prioritize heart connections and include people in what I do.
11. I receive feedback and make it the norm to share about positives and areas needing improvement.
12. I don't receive negative hearsay shared about other people.
13. I identify and proclaim the unique giftings and attributes I see in the people in my life.
14. I "date" people in smaller things before releasing them into higher responsibilities.
15. I have a leadership training mentality, not a "fix people's problems mentality."

Notes

Authority

1. I carry authority in the spirit realm as a son or daughter of God.
2. I have been given authority from God. (Luke 10:19)
3. I fully trust the Lord and he exalts me at the right time. (1 Peter 5:6)
4. I am confident in the place that God has assigned me to influence others.
5. My words carry authority.
6. People under my authority feel covered and safe.
7. God has given me authority to accomplish the things He has called me to.
8. I am able to motivate and inspire people without using manipulation or intimidation.
9. My authority empowers others with authority.
10. I stay in peace and quiet confidence even when my authority is challenged.
11. I am able to joyfully submit to those in authority over me.
12. I only use my authority to protect and empower others.
13. God always gives me clear direction and wisdom on how to use my authority.
14. I know the rights I have been given through Jesus and go boldly before the Throne of God in prayer.
15. I have authority to resist and defeat any demonic influence in the places God has empowered me.

Notes

Influence Part. 1

1. I carry favor from God to be a leader and great influencer. (Joshua 3:7)
2. My influence is increasing in dramatic ways.
3. I lead confidently because the Holy Spirit leads me. (Luke 12:12)
4. I am strong and courageous. I am not afraid or dismayed for the Lord my God is with me wherever I go! (Joshua 1:9)
5. My influence is growing every day.
6. I influence others in a positive way under the influence of the Holy Spirit in my life.
7. People recognize me as a leader they can trust.
8. People feel safe and valued under my leadership. People want to be led by me.
9. I am confident around powerful leaders and show up completely in who I am.
10. As a leader, I am always empowering the people around me to do what they didn't know they could do.
11. I'm a momentum creator.
12. I am visionary and can see what is possible.
13. I communicate my vision well to those I influence.
14. I am an inspiring person and inspire people with my words.
15. I am a builder of people.

Notes

_____
_____
_____
_____
_____
_____
_____

Influence Part. 2

1. My enthusiasm is a thermostat improving every environment I am a part of.
2. I have an incredible ability to inspire others to walk in perseverance, integrity, and courage.
3. I am a catalyst for personal growth in others.
4. Jesus influenced the world dramatically, and so do I.
5. Just as Peter's shadow caused healing in Acts 5, my very presence releases miraculous transformation to those around me.
6. There is no limit to the types of people and situations I can impact.
7. My life causes multitudes to be born again and to bring transformation.
8. My influence will be felt for hundreds of years.
9. My descendants will be great leaders and influencers.
10. I value and understand the needs of people; therefore, I have great favor and influence.
11. My hope, finances, strategies, and partnerships with others are causing great positive change in lives and nations.
12. It is impossible for people to be around me and not be changed.
13. I am so full of Holy Spirit that people get accidentally healed and set free just walking by me.
14. My prayers change everything! (James 5:16)
15. My positive influence increases dramatically every year of my life.

Notes

Character

1. I am a person of my word, and I follow through on what I say I will do. (Matthew 5:37)
2. People trust me because of how I live my life.
3. I am a person of consistent character and integrity.
4. I do the right thing even when it costs me in finances, popularity, or career advancement.
5. I make great choices that are in line with integrity and godliness.
6. I am honest in every area of my life.
7. I run from temptations and will not entertain doing wrong.
8. My words accurately reflect my heart and mind.
9. I refuse to make compromises in my finances, obligations, or relationships.
10. I am the same person in public as I am when I am alone.
11. I avoid situations that would even appear like a compromise. (1 Thessalonians 5:22)
12. I see challenges and difficulties as opportunities to develop my character further.
13. I do not make compromises for personal gain.
14. I follow through on all of my commitments.
15. I am quick to take responsibility for the decisions and mistakes I have made.

Notes

_____
_____
_____
_____
_____
_____
_____

Meetings I Lead

1. I am a leader of powerful meetings.
2. I thoroughly enjoy preparing for meetings, and I am ecstatically confident in my ability to lead them.
3. People in my family, church, and organization know they will encounter God's love, goodness, and power in the meetings I lead.
4. Every meeting I lead is significant and key to the success of my organization.
5. I successfully lead diverse kinds of people in meetings.
6. I carefully consider the input from all those on my team.
7. I have great wisdom in dealing with problems and unexpected happenings in the meetings I lead.
8. More is always accomplished in my meetings than what was on the agenda.
9. I do not over-plan meetings but leave room for unexpected good and needed happenings to occur.
10. People feel safe in the meetings I lead, and they feel they can be honest in sharing their perspectives and feedback.
11. I speak well and am able to articulate my thoughts.
12. I move things forward in meetings without being stress and frustration.
13. I am good at recognizing what God is doing in the middle of meetings.
14. I always value people above the agenda in the meetings I lead.
15. People eagerly desire to be a part of the meetings I lead.

Notes

_____
_____
_____
_____
_____

OUR CHURCH

Favor In Our City

1. Our city knows our church because of our love. (John 13:35)
2. Our church is like salt, influencing every part of the city we live in. (Matthew 5:13)
3. Our church brings light to dark places. (Matthew 5:14-16)
4. Our church is creating a revolution of love.
5. The city leaders see our church as an asset to the city.
6. We are invited into helping the city meet the needs of the people.
7. Our church is bringing restoration into the places of brokenness in the city.
8. We are spoken well of by people in the city, and well respected.
9. Other churches in the city love to partner with us to bring hope to our city together.
10. Our church is seen as trustworthy and as having high integrity.
11. Our church is pursued for solutions to city challenges.
12. Everyone comes under God's favor when interacting with people from our church.
13. Our church is seen as a voice of hope for how the city can improve.
14. Our church is growing in favor with God and with man.
15. Our church invests into the city because we love our city!

Unity

1. Our church is firmly connected to one another with love. (Colossians 3:14)
2. Our church lives in unity and God commands a blessing over us. (Psalm 133:1)
3. Our church recognizes the strength of what each member brings. (Ephesians 4:16)
4. We quickly forgive one another. (Colossians 3:13)
5. Our love for one another gets the attention of people. (John 13:35)
6. We are slow to speak and quick to listen to one another. (James 1:19)
7. We bear one another's burdens. (Galatians 6:2)
8. Our unity as a church is growing every day.
9. Our church has an unusual ability to resolve relational disagreements.
10. Our church is an honoring community, and we assume the best about each other.
11. We are not afraid of having brave conversations with one another to strengthen our unity.
12. We have a high value of every person no matter their background or position.
13. Our church celebrates each other's victories.
14. We refuse to listen to gossip about others in the Body.
15. We protect our connection with one another, even when we disagree.

Notes

_____

_____

_____

_____

_____

Hunger and Revival

1. I am living in revival and spiritual renewal now.
2. Our church is blessed because we stay hungry and thirsty for righteousness and more of God. (Matthew 5:6)
3. Our church has great spiritual hunger and tenacity which brings great rewards. (Galatians 6:9)
4. Our church is always thirsty for more of God's Presence and power.
5. Our appetite for God increases every day.
6. We live lives of life of great spiritual hunger.
7. We live lives of radical faith.
8. We will increasingly experience every aspect of the salvation that Jesus won for us.
9. Our spiritual hunger and personal revival bring breakthrough to everyone around us.
10. The Church is triumphant. (Matthew 16:18)
11. Our church is known as a revival center, full of power and Christ-likeness.
12. Our church opens doors for radical revival movements that invite the nations to be touched by God.
13. Our church walks in sustained revival.
14. Our leaders and elders have a unique ability to always see where God is moving.
15. We respond quickly to what God is doing, both corporately and personally.

Notes

_____
_____
_____
_____
_____
_____

Serving

1. We have hearts to serve like Jesus. (Matthew 20:28, John 15:13)
2. We are more focused on God's kingdom than our own. (Matthew 6:33)
3. I serve the Lord with gladness. (Psalm 100:2)
4. We use the gifts God has given us to serve others. (1 Peter 4:10)
5. Our church is known for our heart of servanthood, and we have great influence in the Kingdom of Heaven.
6. We do not serve so God will love us, but we serve because we have experienced God's love.
7. We know what areas we are called to serve in, and we know what areas we are not called to prioritize at this time.
8. Our church is a strength to people in their area of weakness.
9. The people in our church look for ways to serve and share their gifts with the Body.
10. The people in our church interact with our church as they would a family.
11. Our church raises up volunteers to help people get breakthrough and fulfill their dreams.
12. Our youth group and children's ministry is known for their giving hearts and spending their time to help others.
13. Our church family naturally lay down their lives for each other.
14. Our church leaders are loved and well-supported in our church.
15. If someone in our city or church goes through a challenging time, there is an army of people ready to support, cover, intercede and give to help.

Notes

Church Finances

1. Our church has an abundance for every good work to fulfill the Great Commission of Matthew 28.
2. The people who connect with our ministry receive financial breakthrough and release financial breakthrough to others.
3. The Lord commands His blessing on our storehouses and in all that we set our hands to do, and He blesses us in the land that He is giving us. (Deuteronomy 28:8)
4. We are God's children and all that He has is ours. (Luke 15:31)
5. We are being made rich in every way so we can be generous on every occasion. (2 Corinthians 9:11)
6. God trusts our church with His abundant, limitless resources.
7. Every person is our church is debt-free and abundantly generous.
8. Our church goes the extra mile in honesty and in establishing accountability concerning how ministry money is handled.
9. Our church is vision-driven rather than needs-driven with our finances.
10. The people in our church are full of hope for both personal and corporate finances.
11. We are in a place of such abundance and overflow that we are able to sow into our community and those in need.
12. We have a high value of generosity, and the members of our church catch that core value in their own lives.
13. Our church is generous in the salaries and benefits for our paid staff.
14. We are known for excellence and beauty in our community.
15. We always leave room for the Lord's input on how to use our finances.

Notes

_____

_____

_____

_____

Leadership Team

1. I believe I am called to serve under the leadership of those over me now.
2. I have honor for those who are placed over me.
   (1 Thessalonians 5:12-13)
3. I thrive under the leadership God has placed in my life.
4. I have favor with my leaders, and I am a valuable part of the team.
5. I have great connections with the other leaders on the team.
6. I assume the best of my leaders and give them the benefit of the doubt.
7. I can fully be myself in total freedom when I'm around my leaders.
8. I have powerful and healthy relationships with my leaders.
9. My leaders recognize my gifts, and my gifts make room for me.
   (Proverbs 18:16)
10. I am free from bitterness and am able to bless the lives, families, and finances of those serve.
11. I love to cover the weaknesses of those who have been placed over me.
12. My leaders walk in integrity, love, and purity.
13. I am good at maintaining high-level beliefs about my leaders even when they disappoint me.
14. I always know what to do and how to think when I disagree with my leaders or they have disappointed me.
15. I support my leaders by intentionally speaking hope, appreciation, and encouragement to them.

Notes

_____
_____
_____
_____
_____

16

SPECIFIC LIFE CHALLENGES

Overcoming The Past

1. My past is being supernaturally turned into something beneficial for others and me. (Romans 8:28)
2. I am not who my past says I am, I am who God says I am.
3. In all things, I am more than a conqueror through God who loves me. (Romans 8:37)
4. Jesus has overcome the world and so have I. (John 16:33, 1 John 5:4)
5. The past does not have the power to block a good future for me.
6. I allow love to go into my past and restructure false conclusions I have made about myself.
7. I allow Jesus' love to cover my sins and restore my true identity.
8. I am free from all shame and guilt because in Christ I am a new creation.
9. I do not deny the past. I just don't get my beliefs from it.
10. My experience is transformed as I believe the truth of who I truly am.
11. God's love and power are healing me from the negative things that happened in my past.
12. I peacefully see my past with compassion and affection.
13. When I look at my life, I see my history with God and how He has pursued me.
14. It is easy for me to let go of things I don't understand in my past and trust the Lord with my life.
15. I am happy with who I have turned out to be.

Unexpected Difficulty/Disappointment

1. God's grace is sufficient for me to make it through any situation in victory. (2 Corinthians 12:9)
2. Jesus is the author and finisher of my faith. (Hebrews 12:2)
3. I believe that He who dwells in me is greater than he who dwells in the world. (1 John 4:4)
4. God is with me and will never leave my side. (Matthew 28:20, Joshua 1:5)
5. God is good all the time, and I trust God's goodness, especially in confusing times.
6. God sent His only son to die for me, so I know he is a good God.
7. God will turn this situation around for good in my life and the lives impacted by it.
8. I have a great perspective of the bigger picture God is doing in my life.
9. I know when to stand in faith against negative happenings, and I know when to rest and simply trust.
10. Great things are ahead for me in my life.
11. I have an unusual ability to overcome regret and shame quickly.
12. I am a thankful worshipper no matter what the circumstances.
13. God has an epic plan for my life, and there's absolutely no way I'm going to miss out on it.
14. I carry complete peace and wisdom when difficult situations arise.
15. Today, the Lord is restoring my soul and making all things new in my life.

Notes

_____

_____

_____

_____

_____

SPECIFIC LIFE CHALLENGES

Lingering Illness

1. I walk in ever-increasing health. (Isaiah 53:3-5, Psalms 103:1-3)
2. The same spirit that raised Jesus from the dead is giving life to my body right now. (Romans 8:11)
3. God heals all of my diseases. (Psalm 103:3)
4. God always shows up when I am battling a long-standing issue.
5. Like Abraham, my hope and faith increase the longer an unfulfilled promise exists.
6. The duration of a problem does not determine the likelihood of my breakthrough.
7. I persevere in seeing miracles happen.
8. I am not discouraged about my future health. I am highly hopeful and expectant for full healing to come, whether through supernatural or medical sources.
9. God is inspiring advances in medicine in this area of sickness that will greatly, positively impact my life.
10. Today is the day of breakthrough!
11. The goodness and glory of God are being revealed through my health.
13. I do not have to earn or work for my healing - it was purchased on the cross and belongs to me!
14. I am overflowing with hope and encouragement at the state of my health.
15. It's easy for me to notice even small improvements, and I am getting better every day.
16. It is the desire of my Father's heart to have me perfectly healed and whole.

Notes

_____

_____

_____

_____

Anxiety/Depression

1. I am free of all worry and anxiety. The peace of God guards my mind and heart. (Philippians 4:7)
2. I give all my worries and anxieties to God because He cares for me. (1 Peter 5:7)
3. Jesus has given me his perfect peace. (John 14:27)
4. God is a shield around me and the one who lifts my head high. (Psalm 3:3)
5. I speak to any worry, stress, or anxiety, and I say you cannot stay. Peace reigns in this temple.
6. I have a unique ability to remain peaceful, even as responsibilities increase.
7. My peace is growing, and it is a great spiritual weapon.
8. My thoughts are free from fear, worry, or anxiety.
9. I do not identify with depression. I am a child of God, and righteousness, peace, and joy are my birthright.
10. I easily take thoughts captive that would lead me into depression or anxiety.
11. Today, I'm powerfully aligning my beliefs with God's to birth joy-filled, victorious emotions in me.
12. The history of my family's mental health does not determine my future. I get to enjoy the heritage and family history of Jesus!
13. I am very emotionally healthy, and I can experience sadness and grief without getting stuck there.
14. Jesus always meets me in places of heaviness and lifts me out.
15. Father God is not afraid or overwhelmed and has the perfect solution for me.
16. The passion and wholeheartedness I carry are beautiful gifts, and I am learning each day how to utilize these strengths.

Notes

_____

_____

_____

SPECIFIC LIFE CHALLENGES

Overcoming Addictions

1. I am completely set free from all addiction!
2. I am not who my past says I am, but I am who God says I am.
3. At the cross I was made a new creation; therefore, I do not have to be influenced by any baggage of the past. (2 Corinthians 5:17)
4. I have been set free and released from all bondage through what Jesus has done for me. (John 8:36, Galatians 5:1)
5. I am free from condemnation, and during temptation I find God's strength working mightily in me. (Romans 8:1, 1 Corinthians 10:13)
6. I am not destined to struggle with the same addictions my parents or grandparents were bound by.
7. Every day I make the choice to walk in the freedom Jesus paid for me.
8. Today is the day of my breakthrough — I am free!
9. Every generational curse was broken at the cross; therefore, I am victorious and free from addiction.
10. I am surrounded by powerful people in my life to help me walk in freedom.
11. I am healed from every root that would cause me to walk in addictive behaviors.
12. I willingly give up habits that are hindrances to the promises of God over my life.
13. I have quality relationships with strong, addiction-free people.
14. My breakthrough will be a catalyst for many others to find freedom in this area of life.
15. I am not motivated to change by shame and guilt, but by the delight of the Father, and He is so pleased with me!

Notes

_____

_____

_____

PERSONAL DECLARATIONS

Tips For Writing Declarations

Steve and Wendy Backlund often say,

"You can't consistently do what you don't believe you are."

Whenever possible, write declarations that are identity statements (ie "I am a powerful leader!").

Write declarations in the present tense (ie "I am free from fear"). Avoid "in process" statements ("I am getting free from fear") and aspiration statements ("I will one day be free from fear").

If possible, give a Scripture reference or even make scriptural declarations.

("God has not given me a spirit of fear... 2 Tim. 1:7). Declarations don't always have to be tied directly to specific verses about your future, but it helps solidify these truths into your spirit.

Consider as many possible lies for the topic that would need a truth declaration made. As you are replacing the lies with truth you may find there are different aspects of the lie you may need to address.

Continue to add new declarations until the truth is firmly established in your beliefs.

PERSONAL DECLARATIONS

Prophetic Words

Below, or in a separate journal or on your laptop, write your prophetic words that you're still waiting to come to pass in your life. Then, turn them into declarations over yourself.

Promises

Below, or in a separate journal or on your laptop, identify promises God has given you personally or in Scripture and turn them into declarations over yourself.

Breakthrough Areas

On the following page, or in a separate journal or on your laptop, identify areas where you're specifically wanting to see breakthrough in your life. Ask God which specific areas He wants to lead you into breakthrough. For instance, you could seek spiritual, relational, emotional, physical (health), or financial breakthrough.

Then, ask God what lies you're believing about each area and write them down, followed by asking Him, "What is the truth?" about each of those lies you're believing.

Write down the truths you hear Him speak to you, along with any Scripture truths that come to mind to combat these lies.

Finally, write declarations based on these truths God gave you to declare in place of the lies you've been believing. Speak these truths aloud for targeted breakthrough in these areas of your life.

DECLARE IT

Areas Where I'm Seeking Breakthrough:

Lies I'm Believing About Those Areas:

What is the Truth?

My Declarations Based on the Truth

PERSONAL DECLARATIONS

Below, or in a separate journal, identify dreams God has put in your heart. Spend some time with Him writing declarations to speak over yourself to bring momentum to these dreams.

Ask God what identity statements He wants you to speak over yourself in regards to these dreams.

MORE RESOURCES

We hope you've enjoyed this collection of powerful declarations! For more on declarations, check out:

Steve's book, *Declarations: Unlocking Your Future*

>Includes 30 biblical reasons for declaring truth over every area of life.

>He also answers common objections and concerns to the teaching about declarations. The revelation this book carries will help you to set the direction your life will go.

>Get ready for 30 days of powerful devotions and declarations that will convince you that life is truly in the power of the tongue.

Steve's book, *You're Crazy If You Don't Talk To Yourself*

>This book reveals the incredible power of words, the necessity of talking to our soul, how words set the course of our life, and how the "hearing of faith" is the key to the miraculous, amongst many other powerful truths.

More Declarations on Ignitinghope.com (ignitinghope.com/declarations/) References to several more sets of free declarations,

MORE RESOURCES

including Spirit Awareness Declarations by Wendy Backlund and Declarations for Kids.

NEGATIVITY FAST POSITIVITY FEAST

Join thousands of others for 40 days of radical mind renewal as we let go of lies and instead feast on God's truth, becoming "transformed by the renewing of our minds". (Romans 12:2)

BELIEFS TRAINING

We have a team of greatly equipped, high-level belief trainers ready to partner with you and the Holy Spirit to help you renew your mind and transform your life.

Beliefs training is designed for three kinds of people:
- Those who want to go from good to great
- Those who want to replace life-restricting lies with truths that will set them free in their emotions and then in their circumstances
- Those who want to learn how to practically renew their minds concerning the emotions and circumstances they face

IGNITING HOPE ACADEMY.COM
Online e-courses include:
- Transformational Mind Renewal Course
- Thriving Church Leadership
- The Culture of Empowerment
- Victorious Emotions

IGNITING HOPE
www.ignitinghope.com

Igniting Hope Ministries on Youtube
@IgnitingHope
Facebook.com/ignitinghope

Join our Weekly Newsletter

Made in the USA
Coppell, TX
08 December 2023